Cupid *on* Trial

ISBN 978-1-7327369-2-4

Library of Congress Control Number
2018910863

Edited by Tami Whitney
and Frederick Johnson at Standout Books

Cover Design by Alexander von Ness at Nessgraphica

Interior Design by John H. Matthews at Book Connectors

Cupid *on* Trial

What We Learn About Love When Loving Gets Tough

Brian Jory, Ph.D.

Foxford International
Books and Media
Atlanta – London - Edinburgh

CONTENTS

PREFACE

It is never easy to love someone, especially if you try to love that person with any depth or for any length of time. We humans are so prone to fear, lust, jealousy, boredom, and arrogance that we sometimes allow these emotions to overpower the love we feel. It takes two to breathe life into a relationship, but it only takes one to smother it, wear it out, or blow it apart. That's the risk you take when you entrust your heart to someone, and that someone is taking the same risk with you.

It's ironic, but the very love that could heal a troubled relationship often ends up a casualty in the battle to save it. We sometimes say that couples drift apart; and it's true that some problems smolder for years. But when relationships come to an end, they often go up in a ball of smoke and fire. Gratitude and goodwill are thrown out the window; things are said and done that can't be taken back. The fallout can be devastating, especially when there are children involved. Those who have been through a difficult breakup know exactly what I'm talking about; those who haven't can count themselves as lucky.

When loving gets tough, your hopes and dreams may be hanging by a thread; everything you believe about yourself and your partner can end up teetering on the edge. We strive to make our relationships work—virtually everyone wants a secure relationship with someone they care for, who also cares about them—but in this day and age, it's getting harder and harder for couples to create this kind of intimacy and sustain it over time. Too many end up wondering what went wrong or find themselves living in a hollow shell, residing together but living alone. And there's no pill harder to swallow than *if only* or *what could have been.*

I've spent many years researching relationships, teaching about intimacy, and counseling couples, and I don't think it has to turn out this way. I've written *Cupid on Trial* to explore what it means to love and be loved in our contemporary times, including what it means to love yourself. This book comes out of my conviction that it is never too early—or too late—for couples to plan a happy ending.

My line of work takes me into deep, delicate places— into the thoughts and feelings of men and women who are learning to love—on the job and without an instruction manual. Over the years, I've logged thousands of hours with couples, experiencing along with them the joy, peace, conflict, and betrayals of intimacy. I've studied videos of their heart-to-heart conversations and verbal conflicts, created questionnaires to tap into their hearts and minds, and designed exercises to help them understand what they want out of life and expect from one another. I've had

BRIAN JORY | iii

frank discussions with couples about their intimate sexual desires and helped them speak honestly and openly with one another about what they need—without fear or shame.

Through my work, I've been an eyewitness to love's triumphs and tragedies—all the while keeping records of everything from the inspirational and romantic to the boring and mundane. I am a bearer of couple's stories, and the volumes of stories entrusted to me tells a story of its own about what works in love and what usually doesn't. My knowledge comes from real couples—and their stories comprise the book you are holding in your hands.

Every couple has a story, and it usually begins with how they met. *Cupid on Trial* is a collection of love stories, but they are not all sunshine and roses; these stories tell of love in turbulence, relationships pushed to the brink, and lovers in situations they never saw coming. Some are feel-good stories with happy endings; others are like accidents you can't look away from. They're not fairy tales; they're about love as we experience it in the real world—joyful, painful, sometimes dramatic, sometimes quiet—and as you read you will feel all their emotions and more. These characters live as we live, love as we love; you'll find in each story the candid experiences of lovers who understand the meaning of "when loving gets tough." Every story is based on real events, but the characters are fictionalized to protect their privacy.

As humans, we learn from stories—our own and those of others. You will adore many of these characters; they are heroes. Others you will not like at all. Love or hate, I promise that you will learn important truths about yourself from them. Think of the stories as object lessons, cautionary tales, or parables, and breathe a sigh of relief that you're learning from the mistakes and misfortunes of others and not your own.

Here's a quirky fact: a million people a day ask Google, "What is love?" So take comfort in knowing that you're not alone. These people aren't stupid; they know that love isn't something you order off of Amazon or pick up at Target. They're asking Google because who we can love and how we're supposed to express it have changed dramatically in recent times—practically overnight. We're struggling with questions about love, intimacy, and sexuality that didn't exist in our parents' generation. We're sending messages, lots of them, but are we really communicating? We're sharing sexy photos and videos, but is this the kind of intimacy we really want? All this is to say that you can't blame people for turning to Google: we have to get help wherever we can find it. It's the wild, wild West out there.

So I made up my mind to write about what love means now, in contemporary times. And that's what *Cupid on Trial* is about: what is love? What is the fluff and what is the real deal?

I wanted to create a fresh vision of love and intimacy, something different from the past and more applicable to our day and age. So I started with the idea that love is a form of power, a natural force encoded in our genes. Love is dynamic and ever-changing; it flows within us, between us, and around us. It moves, drives, transforms, bonds, collides, and even repels at times. It can flow in two directions or just one, and the direction can change in the wink of an eye. Love can multiply our combined forces exponentially, or it can seep and dwindle into nothing. In *Cupid on Trial*, you won't find the old-fashioned idea that a relationship is simply a case of choosing the right person and settling down to hibernate; instead, a relationship involves making choices every day about how to use, control, and guide the power you already have.

It's easy to see the power of being loved—being loved and cared for makes us happier and healthier; we even live longer. Those are proven facts, and we see them all around us in couples who nurture and care for one another, listen to and affirm one another, plan together, and challenge each other when necessary. We see the power of being loved in happy bedrooms, healthy kitchens, positive parenting, emergency rooms and treatment centers of all kinds. That's not news to anyone, I hope.

As my studies progressed, however, I came to realize that love isn't simply a force in the lives of those who are loved—it's even more powerful in the lives of those who choose to love. In fact, who we choose to love, and how we choose to express that love, may be the single most powerful force in any of our lives. Choosing to love breaks us free of lonely anonymity in a vast universe. It brings meaning, purpose, and structure to our lives; it transforms us, molds and shapes us into the most powerful versions of ourselves we can be. The transformation can be a slow burn over decades, but it can also be quick and long lasting. It's a strange twist, but giving love to someone isn't necessarily giving; it's just as much taking.

My studies discovered something more, though, and this lesson should be taken as a warning: like any natural force, love that is misdirected or allowed to spiral out of control will wreak havoc on the naïve and unwitting, and will bring those who are careless with its power to their knees. Running rampant, love has been known to leave scorched earth and bodies in its wake. Through my studies, I came to see that we manage love with our beliefs—they're the only tools we have for the job. Believe you are strong, and you will be; believe you can overcome, and you very well might. Believe in respect, and your love flies in one direction; lose respect and it goes into a tailspin. Make yourself accountable and take a smooth ride; take your partner for a ride and see how far you get. Learn to forgive and you will overcome obstacles; hold grudges and watch the darkness settle in. In love, we go the extra mile to be careful—trying to never be careless or carefree.

So we start *Cupid on Trial* with the idea that love always changes us, both in the giving and the receiving, and that a relationship demands new choices day in and day out. Over time the choices we make mold and shape us into who we are and who we want to become. Nobody is perfect; we make our choices carefully, as best we can, with the information and knowledge we have available. You will see these ideas from cover to cover. As you turn the pages, you will witness what happens to those who choose wisely—and those who don't.

WELCOME TO LOVEJOY

Let me be the first to say hello and welcome you to Lovejoy—a living, breathing city created for you to learn about love in our contemporary times. Make yourself at home; you're here to be entertained and educated. Eavesdrop in our kitchens, living rooms, and bedrooms. Listen in on conversations at the Coffee Bean Café. Share in our secrets. Comb through our minds. Let yourself feel our feelings. Consider how you would act in our predicaments. Meet our beautiful children, but remember, this book isn't for kids. We try to shield them from our adult drama; they don't need to know about our struggles. Couples in Lovejoy are like couples everywhere, so try to keep an open mind, and don't judge too fast.

One thing I ask, dear reader, is that you read with an attitude of self-reflection. If you're new to the idea, self-reflection is easy. As you read, become aware of yourself. Think carefully about yourself and how you treat your partner. Then ask yourself whether you would want to trade places with your partner? In other words, what is it like being in a relationship with you? Don't answer that question too quickly; give Lovejoy a chance to make an impact before you come to any conclusions. If you insist that you are easy to love, you can bypass Lovejoy completely. Put this book down—you won't like it. Cupid on Trial isn't for the over-confident; it's for those who are rough around the edges and looking for a better way.

When you turn the page, you'll be welcomed into the home of Liliana and Charlie and many other couples. Some of these couples are friends and neighbors, some are family, others work together. A few keep their distance, and you will soon understand why. Just remember, the story isn't over until you reach The Happy Ending. Whatever you do, don't forget to self-reflect. Now let's turn the page: Lily is waiting and she's hurting. Let's check in on her now.

BE STRONG

The Powder Keg

It's three in the morning, and a shadow slinks out of the ceiling above Liliana's bed, slithers down the wall, and spreads across her as if it wants to smother her. She pulls the blanket over her head, but suddenly too hot, rips it off again. She shivers in a cold sweat. Her breast burns like someone put a blowtorch to it. Memories begin to gnaw, and she grinds her teeth as if to bite them back. She props herself up on a pillow and looks at Charlie, who is sleeping like a baby alongside her. She reaches over to wake him, but thinking better, pulls back. She lies down and whimpers alone until she falls asleep.

The next morning, Liliana follows Charlie down the hall as he heads out to the office. "I was wondering if you'd go on a date with me," she barks from behind, loud enough to get his attention but tentative enough that it doesn't even sound like a question.

He does a 180 and looks her up and down. "Your pajamas are drenched."

"I didn't sleep well."

"You mean, like a date-date? Just the two of us? Why?"

"Why not? They call it 'date night' when you're married. It might be fun."

"Is it a special occasion or something?"

"No, I just thought it might be fun."

"Like when?"

"Like tonight," Lily rattles off the top of her head.

Charlie mulls it over. "All right." Then he takes off down the stairs, and yells, "I love you" as he heads out the door. Liliana goes about getting Dante and Pauli off to school, and later that morning, lines up a babysitter, does her hair and nails, and pulls a blue party dress out of the closet.

When evening rolls around, she and Charlie are off to The Powder Keg, an upscale dance club on the west side of Lovejoy. Charlie orders his usual: Jack Daniels straight, Coke on the side. Liliana is in a mood to try something different; she's not sure what it is, but she orders a Dark and Stormy. After they've both gone through a couple drinks, the DJ cues up "I Gotta Feeling." The music is pumping, and she asks Charlie to dance. He doesn't say no, so they hit the dance floor. It feels good to relax—just what the doctor ordered. Charlie appears to be letting go, too, and Liliana wonders why she didn't come up with the idea of 'date night' a long time ago.

Then the DJ mellows it down with "I See Fire"—a slow dance—and again, Charlie says he'll do it. She buries her head in his chest, and feels safe—for the first time in a long time. Halfway through the song, Charlie gets a text message from work. "I have to respond to this," he says.

So they go sit down. Then there is another message. And another.

Soon Liliana is sipping her Dark and Stormy, watching Charlie text with Alexa.

She excuses herself and weaves her way through the cleavage and short skirts to the restroom, where she heaves her dinner in the toilet. "Sorry, girls," she yells, then locks the stall and sits down.

When she gets back to the table, Liliana can no longer hold it back. "Let's go outside," she shouts over the music, and Charlie follows her through the flashing lights and shimmering bodies to the parking lot, where she lets go. "For a year now, I've watched you get cozier and cozier with Alexa. Late nights. Weekends. Overnight trips to visit clients. I haven't been in a position to say anything, but now I have to tell you how I feel: your relationship with that woman is destroying us, and it's going to destroy the business."

"Don't be petty. The company has soared since I brought Alexa on board. I couldn't get anything done without her. If anything, she keeps the business going."

"Monkey business!" exclaims Liliana.

"What?"

"You heard me. Monkey business. Do you think I don't see how your face lights up when you talk about her? Do you really believe I don't notice that your phone goes dead when you're with her?"

Charlie points his finger. "I love you, Lily. But you know what a cut-throat business film production is. I'm the CEO now. Stay out of it and let me run the business my way."

"Alexa Arioli is your employee. You hired her for marketing and suddenly she's your personal assistant, shadowing you everywhere. The boundaries between you and her have to be clean and above question. The employees have to trust you. You can't get this close to her and not expect ramifications all through the company."

"What are you talking about?"

"I'm talking about her parading her breasts up and down the halls, inviting co-workers to squeeze her new implants. You put your stamp of approval on that. You should have reprimanded her and anyone who laid a hand on her. If she wants to show off her new boobs at home, that's her business. But you can't let the office turn into a sleazy sex club."

"It was all in fun. A girl who likes to have fun can be an asset in the world of film production. I don't see the problem."

Liliana looks at the car valets, who are listening to the whole conversation, and softens her voice. "I'm not trying to tell you how to run the company. I want you to succeed, but I want us to be happy again. Can't you see what a problem this is? You defend her every time. You talk about her all the time."

"Your jealousy is getting the best of you."

"Charlie, if you love me like you say you do, don't go there. If you're lying about Alexa, please stop. I'm begging you. If you've been sleeping with her, or trying to sleep with her, tell the truth and we can work it out together. I can't go on like this; it's killing me."

Charlie takes a deep breath. "Of course I love you. I married you, didn't I? But I have to tell the truth. I can understand why you would be jealous of Alexa, given all your problems. Sure, I spend a lot of time with her. She's easy on the eyes. She's fun. That's not a crime on her part. She's the best personal assistant I could find. She keeps me organized and keeps my stress under control. On the other hand, I get stressed out every time you fly into one of these jealous tantrums. So now I'll beg: please, do we have to keep talking about this? Because I have work to do. I have a business to run."

Liliana can't bring herself to say another word. So they go back inside, and for the rest of the evening, Liliana sips on a Dark and Stormy while Charlie texts Alexa.

It's a quiet ride home. Later that night, Liliana relives 'date night' blow by blow. *Of course I love you. I married you, didn't I?* She plays every word out of Charlie's mouth again and again. She grinds her teeth. Her eyeballs throb. Eventually, exhaustion overtakes her and she falls asleep.

The Meat Counter

Morning rolls around and Liliana flies out of bed, startled by the alarm. She has to cart the kids to school, do her grocery shopping, and make it to an appointment with Dr. McDowell at noon. She sheds her drenched pajamas, pulls on some sweatpants and a heavy sweater, and hurries down the hallway where she comes face to face with

Charlie. She flattens her back against the wall to get out of his way, but as is his habit, he pecks her on the cheek as he heads into the bedroom. "You might want to get your hair done soon. Oh, and sorry about last night. I never know when I'm going to be needed at the office."

Liliana slugs down the stairs.

"Mom, we're going to be late!"

She checks the time as Dante and Pauli pile into the car, and off they go. They pull into the drop-off line at Lovejoy Elementary, and Liliana returns the polite smiles of the other mothers with a polite smile of her own. Occasionally one of them asks a sincere "How are you?" but for the most part, these women don't ask. It's for the best. Liliana has no good answer, and everyone is always in a hurry to get somewhere.

When she gets back from the school run, the house is empty. But she locks the bathroom door behind her anyway. She stands in front of the mirror, takes a strand of hair between her fingers, and studies it. *The color is nice. It's not as thick as it used to be, but it's better than it was. What does he mean, "you might want to get your hair done"? I just had it done.*

She traces a line down each side of her torso with her index fingers, starting with her armpits and heading all the way to her waist. Her fingers meet at her belly-button, and she traces up over her stomach and outlines the shape of her breasts, which are buried beneath her sweater. Then she hits the shower. *Who am I kidding? Charlie hasn't touched my tits in over a year. I'm a hag.*

At the supermarket, Liliana pushes the cart down Aisle 11, and here they come: Dizziness. Heartburn. Nausea. She clutches the cart and tells herself to keep going. But at the U-turn into Aisle 12 she can't seem to turn away from the meat counter. Through the glass partition, she sees butchers decked out in their white coats, trying to stay warm in the refrigerated air, their knives cutting and slicing.

Dr. Brendan Murphy whips a black marker out of his pocket—the same marker that butchers use to mark their cuts—roast here, sirloin there. He draws his lines across her body matter-of-factly. "I'm going to make an incision here. And another one here. Someday you're going to thank me for carving you up like this."

Lily plows her cart into the meat cooler, and blurts out, "I'm not a slab of meat!"

A shopper touches Liliana's arm. "Are you okay?"

Liliana blinks and peers into the shopper's face. "I'm okay, yes, I am okay. And I'm sorry. I'm really sorry." Liliana abandons the cart and rushes to her car. Inside, she locks the doors, and sits, her heart racing, her breathing ragged.

Peppermint Tea

A half hour later, Liliana arrives at Dr. McDowell's office, so sapped of energy that she uses both hands to push the door open. She collapses into a waiting room chair, and does what she always does in Dr. McDowell's waiting room: she picks up a tattered *National Geographic* magazine and buries her face in a story about ape mating practices. Pictures of copulating primates have been a calming influence on Liliana every second Thursday for the past year.

Soon, a nurse emerges and summons her to an examination room Liliana knows only too well. She sits on the examination table and offers her arm.

"How are you, Maria?" she asks the nurse.

"I'm supposed to be asking you that question," Maria replies.

"I'm having a terrible week. Those self-confidence exercises are not helping. Standing in front of a mirror staring at my naked body makes me hate myself even more. They're stupid."

"I'll mention it to Dr. McDowell, but be sure you bring it up with him, too. Your blood pressure is sky high. Do you want some peppermint tea? I just made some."

"Thanks, but I don't really want any tea." After a pause, Lily asks, "Maria, how does your sister like working at Macklin Media?"

"She says she likes it."

"You know your sister pretty well. This is a touchy question, but do you know anything about her fooling around with my husband? I've never brought it up to you, but I have to ask."

Maria stares and swallows hard. "Wow. I'm the wrong person to ask, Lily. I don't know anything about my sister. Nothing whatsoever. Do I think she would get involved with your husband? No. No, I don't think she would. But

I swear, I don't know anything."

"I'm sorry to put you on the spot. I'm carrying a lot of baggage these days. It won't be brought up again."

"No problem, but I hope you find peace soon."

"You know, I've changed my mind. Peppermint tea sounds perfect."

Maria goes out the door, and returns fumbling with a cup of tea.

Dr. McDowell comes in and finds Liliana sipping her tea. "I hear you hate the self-confidence exercises. What do you think about when you look at yourself?"

"The same thing I always think about—my husband. He is making some terrible decisions with our business."

"You're talking about Charlie and Macklin Media?"

"You remember. We edit sound for television and movies. I'm sure you've seen some of them. Do you ever watch *The Walking Dead*?"

"I have a parade of walking dead in here every day; I don't need to watch 'em on television."

"Ha, I'm probably one of them," Liliana laughs.

"Your blood pressure is through the roof. Let's get back to what's agitating you."

"I think Charlie may be having an affair with a girl who works for the company. I'm not naming names. But I'm worried that he's going to get the company sued for sexual harassment. And if he is having an affair, that can't be good for employee morale, either."

"You're worried about Charlie hurting the company? Shouldn't you be worried about how he is hurting you?"

"Hurting Macklin Media is hurting me. My father spent twenty-five years building that company, and when he retired, he gave the lion's share of it to me and Charlie. If anything happens to the company, I couldn't look my dad in the eye. He's counting on me."

"What does Charlie say about it?"

"Oh, he assures me that he loves me. He thinks I'm paranoid."

"Well, are you?"

"I don't have a voice even if I am. I had to get out of the business when I got sick. Charlie took over as CEO, and that's when he made Alexa his personal assistant. He's running the company now, and I have to let him do it his way. I have to be careful about what I say."

"You can't talk to him about this?"

"I tried to talk to him last night, but he doesn't give a shit what I think anymore. He says I'm jealous. I'm this. I'm that. The problem is always me. But he will not shut up about this Alexa. She's gorgeous, and I don't think he can control himself. There's something about her—she's too sexy for her own good."

"I understand that you don't want to lose your business—"

But before he finishes his thought, Liliana's eyes glaze over: *"The biopsy shows a stage four malignancy and the tumor is fairly large," Dr. McDowell says. "I'm going to refer you to a new surgeon in the building, Dr. Brendan Murphy. He's young, but he has a good reputation for knowing the latest techniques. Prepare for the worst, Lily. You're going to lose your breast. But it's lose your breast or lose your life."*

"I don't want to lose my breast!" Liliana shouts. The air is sucked out of the room as Dr. McDowell stares at Liliana and Liliana stares back.

Guardedly, Dr. McDowell says, "Lily, I said, I understand you don't want to lose your business, not 'your breast.' You're having flashbacks about your mastectomy, aren't you?"

Liliana melts into tears. "I can't go on like this. I feel hideous—I'm not a woman, I'm a hag. Why did this happen to me?"

"Grief is natural after losing a part of your body. It's okay to not be okay."

A dam bursts, and the suffering that has been holding Liliana hostage begins to spill. "First, I lose my breast. Soon I will lose my husband. Next, I'm going to lose the business my father devoted his life to. I've lost everything."

"You haven't lost everything. You're one of the lucky ones, Lily. You still have your life. And your boys."

"I am useless to the boys. And my life belongs in a trash can. There's no other way to look at it."

Dr. McDowell sighs. "Look, I said it's okay to not be okay. But it's not okay to stay that way. Look at it like this. The first half of your life was easy, and you took it for granted. You went to college, got married, and had your babies. You played by the rules; you followed the program. Then along came cancer. I told you at the beginning of this: cancer changes everything. Lily, you're trying to put your life back the way it was, but your life will never be the same again. You still have a chance to live your life, but you won't know what life holds for you until you let go of the past and give your future a fighting chance."

"I'm too beat up to try."

"Lily, all cancer has done is make you human. Humans fight to survive. If you quit fighting, you might as well be in a trash can. You're counting on Charlie to make your future, but maybe he's not up to the job. It comes down to you now—your life will be what you make it. So be strong. And when you feel weak, act like you're strong. Try to remember that."

"Remember? Are you joking? Half the time, I can't remember what day it is."

"Then start writing things down. It's simple: B-E S-T-R-O-N-G. What you believe is what you will do. So write it down and believe it. Promise me you'll remember this."

"Okay, I promise to try. But promising is one thing, keeping it is another. I'll do my best."

Powerhouse Tattoos

Liliana leaves Dr. McDowell's office and drives across the parking lot, where she comes to the first choice of her new life: turn left or right? She knows exactly where a right turn will take her—home for a nap before she picks the boys up from school. But a left turn?

A car behind her honks. Her body is begging: *Come on Lily. Go home and sleep for a couple hours. Your bed is your sanctuary.* Then *Be Strong* flashes in her mind. She puts her foot on the gas pedal and turns left.

She drives until she comes upon the Coffee Bean Café. She knows the place—people call it the Starbucks of

Lovejoy. She parks and walks across the street toward the Coffee Bean, trying not to end up crushed beneath a bus or something. Although there have been days when she fantasized about getting run over. She has even rehearsed her final words: "Don't bother to call an ambulance."

At this moment, though, everything feels different. *Be Strong* is echoing like a mantra inside her, along with *What I believe is what I will do*. So, as she starts into the Coffee Bean, she changes her mind, walks past, and goes into the shop next door—a shop she has driven past a hundred times, never once paying the least attention to it.

She walks in awkwardly, pretending she might be in the wrong place, in case she decides to bolt. Inside, a petite woman with mousy-brown hair and a baby bump sits behind the counter. "Need help?" she bellows.

Do I need help? Liliana drifts off into the question for a moment, rolling it around in her mouth as if tasting it. "Um, can I get a tattoo here?"

The pregnant girl lights up. "The sign says Powerhouse Tattoos so I've got a feeling you're in the right place, honey." She waddles around the counter and reaches out her hand. "I'm Aoife Murphy."

"Eefa," Liliana parrots. "What a pretty name. Is it Irish?"

"My great-great-great-grandparents came to America on a famine boat; we have relations in Ireland who love to come visit. We're happy when they come—and happy when they go. What's your name?"

"Liliana. Just Liliana."

"Nice to meet you, Just Liliana," exclaims Aoife with a

big grin. "If you're wondering why I'm so happy, I found out this morning that my baby is a boy. We've decided to name him Ciaran. We spell it the Irish way, C-I-A-R-A-N, but you say it Keeran."

"My, you really are Irish." Liliana realizes she has been holding the girl's hand through the whole exchange. Aoife hasn't flinched a bit, but Liliana lets go, feeling a little embarrassed.

"Do you know what you want, or do you want to look around?"

All four walls are plastered with photos of tattoos. Tattoos on shoulders. Backs. Arms. Legs. Ankles. Wrists. Breasts. Penises. Butts. So many choices. Dragons. Fairies. Animals. Cartoons. Celebrities. Witches. Demons. Vampires. Ropes, braids, vines. Religious symbols of all kinds.

"I know what I want," says Liliana, feeling mysteriously confident in the presence of this angel, Aoife.

"You're ahead of the game then. Fill out the paperwork, and Aiden will be with you shortly. Aiden is our tattoo artist. And my new husband. And soon to be the father of Ciaran. He's Irish, too, and a genius. I'm completely non-biased when I say the man has a gift."

Liliana envies Aoife's devotion. She peers down at the paperwork. First, she fills in her name: Liliana Coscarelli. But the next question, *Have you ever had a tattoo?* paralyzes her.

Dr. Brendan Murphy is measuring her breast—what is left of it at least. "I'm going to put a tattoo here, a dot the size of a dime, to show the radiation therapists where to aim the radiation each time you come in."

She feels in hell. Then, a loud voice: "I hear you want

a tattoo." She snaps back to the present to see a good-looking young man with a curly, reddish beard, something out of *Game of Thrones*. Liliana takes to him immediately. "I'm Aiden Murphy. By now, I'm sure you've heard that I'm a genius," he says, rolling his eyes at Aoife.

"I'm Liliana." She offers her hand in the hope that Aiden will hold it like Aoife did. He squeezes it, but releases quickly.

"Come back to the consultation room and we'll talk about what you want."

In the fog of her flashback, Liliana has managed only to scribble on the questionnaire, and she pulls it back to keep Aiden from seeing her mess. "I'm afraid I haven't finished the paperwork yet."

"No worries; you can fill out the forms later." In the consultation room, Aiden picks up where the questionnaire left off. "Have you had a tattoo before?"

Liliana takes a deep breath. "I was diagnosed with breast cancer last year, and my surgeon tattooed a small dot on my chest to aim the radiation treatments. So I guess you could say I have a target tattooed on my chest. I've never shown it to anyone—not even my husband—but you can look at it if you want to."

Realizing what she has said, Liliana turns red in the face. So does Aiden.

"All I need to know is whether you had an allergic reaction to the ink," he says after a pause.

"No. I had horrible reactions to the radiation itself—that's normal, they tell me—but the tattoo was a breeze."

"Good enough."

"By the way, my surgeon was Dr. Brendan Murphy. Are you related to him?"

"He's my brother. So you were in good hands."

"Well, your brother's hands took my confidence away from me. Maybe your hands will give it back."

"If you know what you want, and it's not too complicated, I can do it right now. Or do you want to go home and think about it?"

"I've thought about it long enough." For reasons she doesn't understand, Lily is magnetically attracted to this man. She would let him tattoo anything he wants on her, anywhere he wants.

One hour later, sporting a brand-new tattoo, Liliana shares a three-way hug with Aoife and Aiden, as if they've been friends forever. "Bye, bye, Just Liliana!" exclaims Aoife. "Let us know how what's-his-name—Charles or Charlie or whatever your husband calls himself—likes your new tattoo."

"Best wishes to you guys, and to baby Ciaran, too. We'll meet again, I'm sure."

Liliana blows them a kiss, and waltzes out of Powerhouse Tattoos just in time to pick up Dante and Pauli from school. For now, her tattoo is her secret. She takes the boys home, and doesn't say a word.

Quite a Night

That night Liliana prays for a good night's sleep, but as Charlie lies sleeping next to her, her body brews up a cauldron of heartburn, sweats, and muscle aches. The world flickers.

She's drugged and strapped to a gurney. In his usual way, Charlie kisses her on her cheek. But in the corner of her eye, Lily sees Alexa standing inconspicuously off to the side, trying not to be noticed. As the attendant wheels Liliana into the surgical cold, the image of Charlie with Alexa stays emblazoned in her mind. It will be the last thing she ever sees if she doesn't come out of surgery alive.

On any other night, this memory might replay twenty times. But now Liliana is working on a promise to Dr. McDowell. She sits up, rolls back her sleeve, and peels the bandage off her new tattoo. There, with moonlight streaming through the window, is a simple note to herself: *Be Strong.*

Liliana is in awe. It's so simple. It's singing to her, guiding her to where she has to go and what she has to do. *What I believe is what I will do.* She slips out of bed, cautious not to wake Charlie. She puts on jeans and a sweater and tiptoes down the stairs, across the kitchen, and into the garage. Now comes the hard part: open the garage door and back the car out without waking Charlie. Every move must be perfect. She backs into the street and double-checks the house. Not a light on anywhere—nothing to suggest that Charlie isn't still snoozing away.

Liliana's heart races along the route to Macklin Media. The streets are quiet this time of night. She pulls into the parking lot and encounters an obstacle she hadn't thought about: the night watchman. Security guards keep records.

If Charlie finds out I was here, he will paint me as the paranoid, crazy bitch he accuses me of being. I need to get back home. I have no business being here in the middle of the night.

Liliana looks to her wrist, and *Be Strong* whispers, *There's no turning back.* She marches up to the security guard, and says, "I need to get something out of my husband's desk."

"No problem, Lily."

"Hey Burt. I didn't expect to see you here. This is like the good old days when I was a kid, romping through these halls."

"Yes, those were good days. They seem like yesterday to me." Burt quickly escorts her to Charlie's office and opens the door. No questions asked.

This puzzles her. "Burt, is it always this easy to get in here in the middle of the night?"

"It's impossible for anyone unless their name is Macklin."

"So?"

"So, your name is Liliana Macklin Coscarelli, isn't it? That makes you the owner. You have access to anything you want around here, any time you want it. Let me know if there is anything else you need."

"Right—of course," she nods, knocked off-balance by the man's words.

Burt returns to his post by the front door. Liliana sits down at Charlie's desk, and stares at the diploma on the wall: *Bachelor of Science in Audio Production awarded to Charles E. Coscarelli.*

He never would have made it through college without me. Lily studies a photo of her and the boys on the bookcase. *Once I was a force to be reckoned with in this place; now I'm a wife in a picture frame. Dr. McDowell was right; cancer changes everything.*

Liliana rifles through Charlie's desk. She finds reports, spreadsheets, memos, and idea boards. Nothing suspicious. *Maybe my jealousy has gotten the best of me.*

Then, in the bottom drawer, she comes across a large, yellow envelope. It's full of something, but it's taped and sealed—no label, nothing written on it. The only way to know what's inside is to tear it open. *If I tear it open, he'll know. But then, maybe that's the idea.* She sits for a long moment. *I need to leave it alone and get out of here.*

But *Be Strong* is firm with her: *You're not going anywhere. You have to open it. It's what you came here for.*

Liliana rips it open, and out falls the mother lode—a treasure trove of greeting cards and love notes passed between Alexa and Charlie. Her hands shake as she scavenges through the pile, now strewn across the desk, opening each letter one page at a time. The *Wanna Get Away?* card from Alexa is a real kick in the teeth; it includes a hand-sketched caricature of Liliana—the evil wife—and a scrawled love scene between her and Charlie. *My Body Aches for You* is another stinger.

Liliana weeps. There's no flashback here; it's real. Faith, hope, and love were all she had, and they are gone.

It's eerily quiet in the office now. She feels peace—she's not a paranoid bitch after all. But the peace is short-lived—the angry despair of betrayal rushes in and takes hold. She grabs her head and wails, "You bastard. You son-of-a-bitch bastard. How could you?" She pounds the desk and swats the pile of letters onto the floor.

Burt rushes in to check on her, but she waves him away. "Leave me alone."

But he doesn't go. "I'm sorry, Lily. I don't want to meddle in your business, but I think I know why you're upset—"

"You have no idea." She waves him away again.

"—You're probably upset over Mr. Coscarelli and Alexa."

Liliana looks right at him. "What do you know about them?"

"I see them here at night."

"You see who here at night?"

"Mr. Coscarelli and Alexa. I know what they do. But you don't have to be here at night to know. It's no secret around the company; folks have known for quite a while. They know they better keep their mouths shut too. Lily, I need this job, but I've known you a long time. I can't keep my mouth shut. Not like this."

Liliana's head floods with the unthinkable. *Has Charlie flaunted his sordid affair in front of everyone? Do employees snicker about her in the restroom? Gossip about her at happy hour? And more importantly, has he stopped to consider that sexual harassment charges against the CEO could bring Macklin Media to its knees?*

An explosion surges through her. *Be Strong* is screaming at her: *You can't be sick anymore. You have to get strong and stay strong. Not next week. Not tomorrow. Now.*

Liliana grabs the cards off the floor, shoves them back in the envelope, and throws it in her purse. She takes Burt by the arm. "Thank you for the truth. You don't know how precious that is to me right now. Let's make a deal for old time's sake, my friend. You didn't see me here tonight. Understand?"

"There won't be any record, Lily. You have my word on that."

"Wish me luck. I have to save Macklin Media."

Wake Up, Bastard

Liliana drives back home along the same solemn streets, but there's a difference now. She hasn't felt this strong in a long time. She's not tired; her mind is clear. She feels a confidence she thought she would never feel again. She pulls into the garage, slips through the kitchen, and heads straight up the stairs. She quietly opens the door of the boys' bedroom and tiptoes in. She stands silently in the shadowed room and watches Dante on the top bunk and Pauli on the bottom. She smells her babies and sighs. She listens to the cadence of their harmonic breathing. Tears seep into her eyes. A lump forms in her throat. She lifts her hand to touch them, but stops short, and backs out of the room without making a sound.

She marches into the master bedroom and stops to take one final look at Charlie's sleeping body. She sniffs the surrounding air and gags. Then she lets out a war cry: "Wake up, bastard!"

Charlie rolls over in a stupor, opens an eye, and, as Liliana dumps the treasure trove on the bed, he moans. "Where did you get this?"

Liliana sits on the chair. "Where do you think I got it?"

"Whoever gave you permission to snoop through my

desk won't have a job on Monday morning."

"This is your last chance to tell the truth, Charlie. Now."

"Okay, here's the truth. You were right; there is a problem with Alexa. The girl oozes sexuality all over the office, and it has caused trouble. I didn't tell you because I didn't want to upset you. I thought I could take care of it myself and keep you out of it."

"After all this, that's the best you can come up with? You don't have a better story than that? What an insult."

"It's the truth. You were right about her all along. I should have listened to you and sent her walking a long time ago. The girl's a slut."

Liliana stands up. "Get your shit and get out. And don't you dare wake up the boys."

"Why?"

"Why? Because I said so!"

"I need to take a shower. Can I take a shower?"

"I said get your shit and get out. Or I call the cops and let them take you out."

Charlie scrambles to throw on some clothes and pack a suitcase. He slinks down the stairs, but turns back at the bottom. "You're making a big mistake. I stayed with you through your problems. No man is going to want a woman with one breast. You'll take me back once you get your head straightened out. Don't do anything stupid."

"As if I would want a man like you."

"You'll want me back. I do love you. You'll figure that out eventually."

Then the doubts set in. *Maybe he's right. Maybe I'm going to be sorry. Don't be so hard on him; he can't help himself.* Liliana glances at her wrist.

"I told you to get out."

Later that day, Lily feels a weight lifted, mysteriously healed and inexplicably strong. She can't seem to stop doing karate chops on any surface that can handle a good whack—the sofa, the dining room table, even the ironing board. Dante walks in the kitchen just as his mom slams a karate chop on the counter.

"Mom, are you taking karate lessons?"

"Not exactly."

"If I gave an answer like that, I'd be in trouble. Is it yes or no?"

"Hmm, good point. No karate lessons. Not yet. But I am doing strength training."

"Mom, are you getting better? Or are you just losing your mind?"

"Honey, I couldn't feel better."

"Don't call me honey, honey." Dante rolls his eyes.

"Okay, baby," Lily counterpunches.

"Where's dad?"

"Out of town as usual. I'm not sure when he's coming back."

"He must have had an early flight. I heard him leave this morning; it was still dark outside."

"Um, he had an early flight alright." Lily pauses to see if Dante says anything more, but he heads to the back yard to play with his brother.

Lily continues to karate chop the counter and dance around the kitchen. *This change happened quickly. How can it be? Of course, things changed fast the day I got the diagnosis. I believed my life was over, and I started feeling sick in a matter of seconds. Now I believe I am strong, and I feel like I can handle anything life throws at me.*

Lily smiles. *What I believe is what I will do. Maybe Dr. McDowell's self-confidence exercises aren't so stupid after all.*

Liliana spends the rest of the day mulling things over. How long will it take her to get rid of Charlie? What will happen to Macklin Media? And how is she going to pay back Alexa? Time is of the essence. She has to get her dad involved and have a talk with the boys. She has to be strong. There's no time for being sick now, and she doesn't feel sick anyway.

Taking Care of Business

Monday afternoon rolls around, and Clark Macklin marches into the board room of Macklin Media, where Charlie Coscarelli is waiting for him. Alongside him is the company's attorney, Danny Coscarelli, who happens to be Charlie's brother. All three are dressed in dark suits and red ties. The pleasantries are short, and Clark begins. "Liliana is running late, so with only two of three shareholders present, this meeting is unofficial. You know why I'm here, Charlie."

"I can guess, Clark. By the way, around here, I am Mr. Coscarelli, even to you. Now get to why you called the meeting."

"I'm here to talk about your role as CEO."

"What about it?"

"Mr. Coscarelli, you were entrusted as CEO to serve the interests of Macklin Media, but you seem to think that the company and its employees exist to serve you. Given the poor judgment you've shown in your affairs, I don't think you're the right person to be at the helm. I'd remove you, but I can't do it without Liliana's vote, so I'm asking you to voluntarily resign."

"It's true. A couple employees have caused problems. Alexa Arioli and Security Captain Burt Lockhart. I have terminated both as of five o'clock today. I have the situation under control, Clark."

Danny interrupts. "Charlie, have you ever heard of sexual harassment? You can't fire Alexa like that. She's going to demand compensation. I'm sure she has a lawyer lined up already. I can't believe you would do something this stupid."

"Forget Alexa; I can handle her," counters Charlie. "It's Liliana we need to worry about. I am going to say this respectfully, Clark, because Liliana is your daughter and my wife. We both love Lily; I know I do. But she has been through a lot in the last year. Since we're talking about poor judgment, breaking in and stealing property in the middle of the night would constitute poor judgment on her part. Wouldn't you agree? I considered calling the police, but you know I wouldn't do anything to hurt Liliana or Macklin Media."

"You know exactly why Lily was here. And you may not

like it, but the fact is that she found what she was looking for," Clark snarls.

Danny chimes in. "Is there proof, or are we talking about rumors and innuendoes?"

"Clark can't prove anything," Charlie says. "And since Liliana isn't here, it's time to bring this meeting to an end. Danny, send your bill to Clark Macklin. This isn't an official meeting, and I didn't ask you to be here today. I'm the CEO of Macklin Media, not Clark. Now, excuse me, gentlemen, but I have a company to run. This meeting is over."

Danny and Clark stare at one another. Charlie rises out of his chair. The door swings open, and Liliana charges in, dressed for business, standing tall and alert.

"Sorry I'm late. I hope I didn't miss anything. Hi Daddy. Hi Danny."

"Are you good?" Clark asks.

"Couldn't be better," Lily replies.

Clark rushes to business. "With Liliana here, I hereby call this meeting to order in accordance with the by-laws of Macklin Media, Incorporated. Let the record show that all three owners are present, and any action taken at this meeting is official and binding. Danny, you are the witness so take notes. The order of business involves the current CEO."

Clark turns to Liliana, "Before you arrived, Charlie was saying that we can't prove the sexual harassment allegations against him."

"Wrong," declares Liliana. She pulls the treasure trove out of her case and tosses it on the table.

Danny grabs a couple of the cards for a quick read. "Come on, Charlie. You and Alexa wrote this shit? And you're blaming your wife? That's real smart, bro. I can't defend you. You're my brother, but you screwed up. Admit it."

"I'm not admitting anything, bro," mocks Charlie.

Clark puts it to Charlie again: "I'm warning you. Step down now. Or we'll put it up for a vote."

"I won't resign. And if you have half a brain, you're not going to vote me out either. Me becoming CEO was the best thing that ever happened to Macklin Media. Income is at an all-time high; profits are booming. And you don't have anyone with my ability to step in. Clark, you're too old. Lily, you're sick. Macklin Media needs me, so whatever your problem, get over it."

"Cast your vote, Charlie, and keep your drama to yourself," says Clark.

"Okay," says Charlie. "As twenty-five percent owner, I vote to keep myself on."

Then Clark votes. "I own twenty-five percent, and I say you're out."

"Lily, don't listen to your dad. A vote against me is a vote to destroy Macklin Media. Are you going to destroy your inheritance? Dante and Pauli's future? Our future? Use your head. Don't let jealousy get the best of you. You know I love you. Vote for me and I promise to make us happy again. Happier than we've ever been. I promise."

Liliana goes glassy-eyed.

I could use a little happiness. This could wreck my life. It could be terrible for Dante and Pauli. Charlie seems sincere—what would it hurt to give him another chance?

Be Strong. Easy to say, but what does it mean right now? This is going too fast. Delay. Smooth it over.

The room is absolutely quiet. Charlie is giving her the evil eye. Her father is staring at her. Danny, too. Lily swallows, takes a breath, and looks Charlie in the eye. "I own fifty percent of this company, and I vote you out, Charlie. And by the way, stop saying I'm sick. You were making me sick. But I'm not sick anymore."

Charlie slams his fist on the table. "You're screwing up. Macklin Media will be out of business in a year without me. Who is going to run this company?"

Liliana turns her eyes to the Macklin Media logo on the wall above her father's head. She thinks about the eighty-five employees who rely on Macklin Media for their jobs. Their futures. Their families.

Lily is eight years old. She is in the sound studio with her father, editing The Little Mermaid. "It's a beautiful movie with beautiful voices, and we have to make the sound perfect," he says. Lily loves Jodi Benson, the voice of Ariel. It all seems like magic to Liliana the little girl. Her dad tells her, "Learn all you can, Lily; one day Macklin Media is going to need you. It's your destiny."

Liliana looks into the faces of the three men who surround her and knows this is the moment. *What you believe is what you will do. You're ready. Do it now.*

"My name is Lily Macklin, not Liliana Coscarelli. I have loved Macklin Media since I was a kid. I'm strong.

I'm ready to come back and lead Macklin Media into the future. I nominate myself as CEO. It's my destiny."

Clark jumps on the bandwagon. "Hell yes, I vote for Lily. My daughter is back."

"I will fight this to the death," Charlie snarls. "You are going to destroy this company."

"Mr. Coscarelli," Clark says, "as Chairperson of the Board of Directors, I hereby inform you that your services as CEO are no longer necessary."

"What about me and Tony? Are we fired, too?" asks Danny.

Clark responds. "You're his brothers, but you haven't done anything wrong that we know of. We'll keep our eyes on you both, but you're still our attorney and Tony's still our accountant—as long as we can trust you. We expect company loyalty, not brotherly loyalty, so don't let us down."

"You and Lily can count on us."

"Charlie, until we buy you out, you will be treated as a silent partner. Get your stuff and get out. The meeting is adjourned."

Is It a Lily?

Liliana stuffs the treasure trove into her case. It's hers now. She exits, but Charlie pushes into her space in the hallway. She turns and points her finger. "Wait here. Security is on their way to escort you out. We'll send your personal belongings tomorrow. Leave an address at the front desk."

"I can certainly find my own way out."

Burt Lockhart comes barreling down the hallway. "You called for security, Lily?"

"I did. Burt, your termination is cancelled; you'll have a job at Macklin Media for as long as you want to work here. Now, escort Mr. Coscarelli directly to his car. If he causes trouble, I authorize you to call the cops."

"Hold on a minute. I want to know something," Charlie demands.

"Yes?"

"What's that on your wrist?"

"I have a new tattoo, that's all."

"A tattoo. You? What is it? A lily? A pretty flower?" He smirks.

"It's a note to remind me of something."

"You're crazy. What does it say?"

"Well, since you asked," she leans into him and whispers, "it says, 'A woman with one breast will whip a man with no balls any day of the week.'"

Charlie stares at her. Burt grabs Charlie's arm, and forcibly drags him down the hall and out the door.

Who Do You Work For?

Danny rushes into the hallway and summons Lily back into the Board Room where her father is still sitting. "We've got trouble here, and I'm not sure how to handle it. What are we going to do with Alexa?"

"Let me handle her," Lily tells the two men.

"Come on, you're not the one to deal with this, Lily."

"Your dad's right. This is a legal problem. Let me work on it."

"I said I am going to handle it," Lily snaps.

Liliana walks down and stands outside the door of Alexa's office, off to the side so as not to be seen. She can't help but reflect on the irony of it all, as she watches Alexa cleaning out her desk. *Wanna Get Away?* and *My Body Aches For You* are crying for justice. *If that little bitch thinks she's going to walk out of here, get a lawyer and a settlement—a nice chunk of change out of my pockets, she'd better think again.*

Finally, she steps inside. "What do you think you are doing?"

Alexa turns and stifles a gasp. She quickly busies herself with the items on her desk. "What do you think I'm doing? Mr. Coscarelli terminated me as of five o'clock today. It's four-fifty. Let me go in peace, and I'll get out of your hair."

"Cut the Mr. Coscarelli crap. We both know he's not Mr. Coscarelli to you."

"You have no idea what he is to me."

"The question you ought to be asking is what are you to him?"

"Maybe the question for you is what am I to him? By the way, I knew this was about to come crashing down. My sister warned me you were asking questions."

Lily purses her lips, and Alexa continues. "I'm no angel, and I don't pretend to be. But if you think I'm taking the blame for what went on here, think again. He came to me."

"Oh, I'm not here to blame you at all; I blame him. Actually, I came by to say thank you."

"Who's peddling the bullshit now? Haven't you heard the talk around here? Alexa Arioli—sleeping her way to the top. Alexa Arioli—home wrecker. Alexa Arioli—slut and whore. I did what I did, but I didn't do it by myself."

"I never thanked you for visiting me in the hospital when I had my surgery. It was a whole year ago, but I haven't forgotten."

"I'm not proud of that. Charlie dragged me into that hospital. I didn't belong there, and I knew it. If it's any consolation, I said a prayer for you. I saw you fighting for your life, and I made your life harder than it already was. For that, I am sorry. I was trying to make my life better, too."

"Charlie is the culprit here—not you. It was his job to treat you with respect. You might have noticed Charlie's not up to the job when it comes to respect. I married him, not you. And who knows? You probably weren't the first. Now, I asked what you were doing."

"I'm packing. Charlie told me to be out of here by five. You know, he called me a slut this morning. All I turned out to be was an easy lay for him."

"I'm sorry that the CEO of this company spoke to you like that." There is a moment of silence, as though nothing more can be said. Then Liliana says, "Alexa, who do you work for?"

"You know who I work for. I'm Charlie's personal assistant."

"Wrong. You're the personal assistant to the CEO of Macklin Media. As of right now, you work for me. And I'm keeping you on if you want to stay. You don't have to go anywhere unless you want to."

Alexa gapes at her.

Liliana continues. "You have a sense of humor, and you're good at getting things organized. I'm going to need all the help I can get whipping this company back into shape. I am asking you to stay on as my personal assistant. I'm willing to give it a try if you are."

The Alexa everyone falls in love with comes alive. "You know, Mrs. Coscarelli, I have spent night after night in bed wondering about you. Truth be told, I thought more about you than Charlie. I'm getting good vibes about you right now. Maybe you and I will hit it off—we certainly have something in common."

"Forget about Charlie," Liliana jabs back.

"Honestly, I don't like Charlie that much. He's as boring as watching ice melt. And he's kind of a user if you know what I mean. And I think you do."

"Plus he's unemployed," chuckles Liliana.

"In the soup line!" Alexa chimes in. It seems as though the party has just begun.

"He's not much in bed, either. Tell the truth."

"Not much to work with down there," Alexa laughs.

"Then it's decided. You work for me, starting right now. We're forgetting the past and focusing on the future. I expect absolute loyalty from you. Don't let me down."

"Yes, ma'am." Alexa salutes like a soldier.

"I am putting my foot down right up front: you're a party girl, and I like that shoot-em-up attitude of yours. But let's get something straight. What you do on your own time is your business. But in this office, you will keep your games under wraps and dress appropriately for a business environment. Do you agree to that?"

"Yes, Mrs. Coscarelli."

"And don't call me Mrs. Coscarelli. I'm not a Coscarelli, I'm a Macklin. Call me Liliana or Lily when it's just the two of us—and Ms. Macklin in public. Got that?"

"Got it, Lily."

"Now, I want you to schedule a company-wide meeting for tomorrow. I want every employee on the payroll there. I'm going to announce that I'm coming back as CEO and assure the employees that there are going to be changes in the work environment around here."

"Consider it done."

"One last thing, Alexa. Bring me a cup of peppermint tea, please. It's been quite a day."

A JOURNAL I ONCE KEPT

Sunday, May 12th

Happy Mother's Day to me! I had an amazing day, and I owe it to Charlie, Dante, and Pauli. We all went to church together—even Mom and Dad. Father Miles gave a sweet sermon about his mother, and all the women got a carnation. I was glad they gave a flower to all the women this year and not just the mothers. It was awkward last year; there were women there who want to be mothers but hadn't succeeded, and I felt guilty taking a carnation. For once, the church is making progress, a little at a time.

After church, Mom was upset—nothing to do with carnations. One of her friends showed up on the prayer list today, diagnosed with cancer. My mom worries about cancer, but—thank God—nobody in our family has ever had it.

We went to *Cucina Emil* for the pasta brunch and I was proud of myself. The boys said, "It's okay to pig out, Mom, it's Mother's Day." But I ordered the vegetarian Linguini and stuck to my diet. Good for me!

Dante and Pauli gave me this journal for Mother's Day and I've promised myself to write three days a week. I've never kept a journal before, but I'm going to try, and three days a week is doable. I hope. Oprah says it's a proven fact that people who reflect on their strengths and weaknesses at least once a week are happier, so if I write three times a week, maybe I'll be three times happier. LOL. I'm going to date every entry to remind myself that this is a day I will never get back, and whatever I make of today (and every day), determines my life. I'm going to end every entry stating one thing I am grateful for. So today was a great day; I wish every day with my family could be this cozy. I am grateful for Charlie, Dante, Pauli, and my mom and dad. They make life worth living.

Tuesday, May 15th

Too good to be true. Charlie bought our tickets for Italy yesterday. We're leaving June fifteenth and coming back on the thirtieth. I'm sure the boys are going to hate the museums in Florence—what do they care about Leonardo Da Vinci? *Is he a footballer, Mom?* I begged Charlie to take us all hiking in Cinque Terre the second week, and at first he said no, so I was shocked yesterday when he said yes. Usually there's no changing his mind.

The boys will like Venice for the boats, and they will be fine hiking in Cinque Terre if Charlie doesn't push them too hard. It shouldn't be too hot on the Mediterranean.

In celebration, I am giving my journal a name. It's *Taste of Italy!* Going to Italy has been on my bucket list for years, so if it's half as good as I hope, it will be a dream come true. I'm cutting this entry short as I am absolutely exhausted. I'd love to sleep in tomorrow if Macklin Media wouldn't fall into chaos without me.

Today I am grateful for Charlie because women ask me how I got so lucky. Sometimes I wonder myself. College footballer, handsome, tall, and dark-skinned. The classic Italian man. I don't say this to my girlfriends, but I think, "Girls, take one look at me: I'm gorgeous, a shapely figure, and perky boobs. Let me show you a few tricks I pull out in bed, and you'll know exactly how I landed Charlie." Tricks every woman should know. Fools if they don't.

Friday, May 17th

Tiring day in the studio. Jane Fonda had to redo lines from *Grace and Frankie*. So full of herself, definitely high-maintenance. That's why I have to work with her. Nobody else can handle her. I asked her to re-do a line and she says, "No. That's as good as it's gonna get." I sucked it up. She runs her own show. Why can't everyone be as nice as Jodi Benson? I love that woman!

So tired lately; pollen season in full swing. I'll pick up some Zyrtec.

Ordered Dante and Pauli clothes for Italy on Amazon. Those Italian girls will be taking a second look at my boys. Red shirts, blue jeans, and Kicks shoes. I miss the days when I could take them to the mall and let them try everything on. Too busy for that, and these clothes will be on the doorstep tomorrow afternoon. Something is lost shopping online, though. Not that my boys care. They'd go in dirty rags if I'd let them. Ripped jeans are in fashion right now, and that's what they want. I said N-O. Italians dress with class, not in holey jeans.

Today I am grateful for Amazon because, honest to God, if I had to go to the mall, walk from the parking deck, eat in that nasty food court, and drag the boys from store to store, I would be exhausted. Something is lost on Amazon, but something is found: a few extra hours of sleep!

Sunday, May 19th

Dante's piano recital was too much. To see him up there in front of so many people, cool and confident, owning the stage... he gets that from his dad, no doubt. I can't believe how calm he was. No mistakes. No childishness. His teacher says she has never had a student take command of his own recital like that. My little boy is growing up and making his mark. I only wish Charlie had been there to see it, but at least Mom and Dad were there to clap for him. I'm sure Dante gets some of his confidence from my dad. These men are cut from the same pattern: confidence is in their genes. They're like rocks! You can't push 'em around or move 'em, and once they're in place, they're there. Flowers will have to grow around them. Why am I off on this tangent?

Charlie got his Sunday round of golf in today, and we had a little skirmish over it. I assumed he was going to Dante's recital. Boy, was I wrong. He missed golf last Sunday for Mother's Day, and he's not going to miss two Sundays in a row. He more or less laid a guilt trip on me: if I wanted him to go to the recital today, I should have let him know last week, and he would have played golf last Sunday. I told him, "Your boys are growing up fast, but you're a grown man, so do what you want." Secretly, I hope he bogeyed every hole; that's karma, baby. He wouldn't tell me if he did.

Today I am grateful for my dad. He showed up for Dante and come to think of it, he shows up for his family more often than not. My dad is a no-nonsense guy with those around him, but he's no-nonsense with himself, too. He doesn't lay any shoulda-coulda-wouldas on others that he doesn't lay on himself. My dad is my rock! Along with Charlie, of course. When he shows up.

Tuesday, May 21st

I don't talk about my mother enough, and I feel guilty about it. I barely mentioned her in my Mother's Day entry, and I don't feel as close to her as she deserves. I resent her. God, did I write that? What kind of daughter resents her mother? Maybe resent is too strong. What I mean is my parents are traditional and old-fashioned, and life seemed simpler back then. My mom got to be the classic Beloved Wife and Mother. I'm pretty sure working outside the home never crossed her mind. She was content to depend on my dad and take a back seat, but was she really in the back seat? I mean, she's lucky. My dad adored her—he still does. At least for all I know. All my mom had to worry about was having dinner on the table at night, fixing up the house, and keeping Daddy happy. No pressure. Something doesn't add up here; it sounds like I'm saying that slaves had it easy because they didn't have choices, they didn't have a mortgage to worry about and they didn't have to make payments on their horse and buggy. That sounds crazy.

It has never occurred to me, but maybe my mom isn't happy. I wouldn't ask her because she wouldn't tell me anyway—that wouldn't be pleasant or polite for a lady to say. Does that mean she's not allowed to speak her mind? She may not even be allowed to know her mind. But what if she likes not speaking her mind? I've got a feeling I could write a book about this and never get to the bottom of it. All I know is that my life is a lot more complicated than my mom's. I guess that's good, because I have choices. But what if I don't want to make choices? What if I want to let Charlie make all the decisions? I am going in circles again? After all, I don't want to depend on Charlie. Do I?

Today I am grateful for choices; even the choices I don't want to make! My thinking on this is cloudy, because in some ways I envy my mom, but I wouldn't want to be her. Comparing my life with hers is comparing apples to oranges. Someday I'll ask her what she really thinks about her role as mom and wife! I'll wait until she's plowed on her afternoon gin and tonics and see if she gets loose-lipped. That sounds like a plan.

Friday, May 24th

Three weeks from tomorrow, we'll be Italy-bound. The boys have their passports now, and their pictures are adorable. It's cute because everybody is the same size in a passport photo, so sure, they have their little boy faces but you can't see how small they really are. I've been studying Italian wines. The boys will get their first chance to drink wine in Italy; that's so long as I don't change my mind once we get there. When in Rome, do as the Romans do—so if kids drink wine in Rome, we'll give it a shot. My guess is the boys won't like it. They don't like communion wine and are always threatening to spit it out. It may be the devil in me, but I'd love to see the look on Father Miles' face if the boys ever do spit wine all over him. God, please don't let that actually happen.

If going to Italy could ever be considered a problem, it's because we are going to four different regions, and the weather in each is different. I'll have to pack the boys' suitcases, and they can only handle so much weight. If there are extra fees at the airport, I'll hear about it from Charlie. That's funny because Charlie's suitcase will be the heaviest. The only difference between him and the boys is size. His will be double the weight of theirs. And no matter how hard I try, he'll complain about what I pack. I don't remember packing his suitcase before we got married and had no idea that "From this day forward" meant packing his suitcase, picking up after him, cleaning the shower after he gets out, buying his clothes, and keeping his calendar. Is marriage a disability for men? The day before the wedding they can do it themselves, and the day after they're disabled. It's Mama Syndrome, and God knows I never do anything like his mother used to.

Today I am grateful for time. I have a lot to do in the next three weeks. This is my vacation, too, and I'm not going to spend all my time playing cook, maid, dishwasher, and transit coordinator for disabled males. I'm still bucking off these allergies: lots of coughing, I'm always out of breath. I could sleep for a week. I'm grateful for 5-Hour Energy, too. It's my rocket fuel.

Tuesday, May 28th

I missed yesterday's entry. No excuse; it was Memorial Day and a nice quiet holiday at home. But today at Macklin Media was a day I'm going to remember for a long time. One of the biggest Italian pop stars of all time is touring the States with an entourage of Italian musicians, back-up singers, and producers. They were swarming the place all day, recording in our studios. His name is Biagio Antonacci, and what a voice! He has sold five million albums since 1998, and two decades later, he still packs stadiums all over Europe. I can't believe I've never heard of him; Americans are so isolated from the rest of the world.

I've never cheated on Charlie and never would, but I swear when Biagio Antonacci started singing *L'Amore Comporta* in the studio, that voice made me want to do things with him you only do in the bedroom—and I couldn't even understand a word he was saying. It wasn't just him either. Italian men are gorgeous, and when they look at you, their eyes pierce into your heart. I was short of breath, but for once it had nothing to do with allergies. I'm not a cheater, but I swear if one of those Italian guys had invited me into a closet, I would have jumped in, no questions asked. Macklin Media was in the erotic zone today, and the women were wet and wild.

Last week Charlie hired a new girl to work in marketing and today was her first day in the office. A group of us were watching Biagio and his backup singers in the control room, practically crying over those pure Italian accents, and the new girl, Alexa, turns to the group and says, "I can't believe I'm getting paid to do this. I would do this job for free with these Italians around. Those tight pants should be illegal." The recording sessions were the best we've done in a long time. Very successful. Sadly, the Italians will be gone tomorrow. But if this is a little taste of Italy, I may never come home.

Today I am grateful for happy feelings. It was nice to hear the pajama-party talk. Hell, let's be honest: it was locker room talk and it was nice to hear it from the girls for a change. Charlie hasn't shown me much attention lately, but Biagio Antonacci made me feel like a hot-blooded woman today. Let me write that again. A woman. Not a mother. Not a wife. Not a daughter. A woman. Italy, here I come.

Thursday, May 30th

I met with Danny and Tony Coscarelli today to go over tax issues they've been talking to the IRS about, and didn't I get a shocker! Now I know why Charlie changed his mind about Cinque Terre. He's having his golf clubs shipped to Italy and Tony and Danny are joining us for a week of golf in Cinque Terre. Bosom brothers playing the links on the Mediterranean while I keep Dante and Pauli entertained and sip wine by myself. I'm more than a little pissed. Finding out from Tony and Danny wasn't cool. I wonder whether I should wait to see how long it takes for Charlie to tell me. Of course, his brothers have probably already let him know they blew the lid off his secret. They were as surprised as I was; they thought they were talking about something I already knew. It's ridiculous. I have no problem with Charlie playing golf with his brothers in Italy—it's his vacation too—what bothers me is that he hides it from me. He's the rock and I'm the flower, as usual. I'm not even going to bring it up to him. What's the point?

Today I am grateful for give and take, unless it's me doing all the giving and Charlie all the taking. Why can't he show a little more respect? What would he think if I pulled this shit with him? I'll bet he doesn't even think about it.

On another note, Zyrtec isn't doing it for me. My allergies have never been this bad. I called Dr. McDowell to see if he could prescribe something stronger, and he wants me to come in tomorrow.

Friday, May 31st

Typical Friday. The new girl, Alexa, is a hoot and she's really taken over the place with her charisma and charm. So much confidence and so funny! It turns out her sister Maria is a nurse in Dr. McDowell's office and the two are very close. Alexa told the wackiest story today about how Maria set her up with a thirty-five year old doctor who says he won't get married until he meets the perfect woman. He has wanted to meet Alexa for two years, but Alexa didn't want to meet him as she was still reeling with a broken heart from her last breakup. She put Maria off and off, and finally, after two years, Alexa and the doctor meet at a party at Maria's. He is good-looking, athletic, great personality, and is well-off financially. Drives a Porsche and a Range Rover. Hey, doctors need love, too. Alexa flips for the guy, and she and the doctor leave together. Maria jumps up and down because she's played Cupid and it's working. Only one problem: next day, the doctor says he isn't interested in Alexa—she isn't his type. Apparently, he can tell this after one evening together. The doctor didn't sink so low as to say Alexa isn't perfect, only that she isn't perfect for him. You had to be there, but Alexa had the room laughing—it was hilarious. She is one wacky fur ball. No wonder she's in marketing; seems like she'll be good for Macklin Media.

Went by Dr. McDowell's office. He asked some questions, and instead of giving me a script, he took my blood. "No give, no take," he jokes. Says he's required to check my blood before he writes this type of prescription. I need a two months' supply to cover me while I'm in Italy. (I presume they have pollen offenders in Italy. Pollen offenders are everywhere! They're taking over the world!)

Today I am grateful for my *Taste of Italy* journal. I had my doubts when I started—thought that maybe it would be a waste of time—but it feels good. I've given up writing on Sunday because Sunday nights are hectic and I like to take my time when I journal. Mondays and Fridays are about right. I'm feeling my journal is a real friend, like it's really mine, someone I trust and confide in through thick and thin. I'm hoping to keep this up for a long time. Going to bed early tonight; peacefully tired.

Afterthought: I am not going to spend all my time journaling negativity about Charlie, because I do love and cherish him, and am grateful to have him in my life. He may be hard as a rock, but a hard man is good to find. I am grateful for his strength. Maybe I am more like my mom than I think: I married a strong man to protect and defend me. A man just like my father. Creepy, but true. Thank you, Dr. Freud.

Monday, June 3rd

Strange day today. Early morning wake-up call from Dr. McDowell. He wants to see me again. I told him, "We've got to quit meeting like this. It's a bit much for a stupid allergy prescription." He transfers me to Maria who tells me his only available time is four o'clock. I promised Marta Kaufman we'd have episode five of *Grace and Frankie* finished by end of day, and it's my day to do the school run. So I ask Maria, "How about I come in tomorrow?"

But Dr. McDowell insists I get in there today.

Charlie. No help on the school run; he's too important to mess with smelly lunch boxes. The neighbor boy puked in the back seat last week and that signaled the end of it for Charlie. I don't like kid vomit either, but I don't like my kids walking five miles home. I track down another mother to pick the kids up and drag in a second engineer to work on *Grace and Frankie*. All of this before I even get to the office, and by the time I get there I feel like taking a nap.

The crazy part doesn't even begin until I get to Dr. McDowell's.

"The gown opens in the front," Maria tells me.

"Why do I need a gown?"

"Dr. McDowell wants to examine you."

"Examine me for what? Allergies?"

"I don't know. Ask him."

Next thing I know, Dr. McDowell has his hands inside my gown, poking my ribs, putting pressure on my stomach, squeezing my breasts.

"How long has that been there?" he says at last.

"How long has what been where? I've had breasts since I was twelve."

"Don't be funny. You've got a cyst or something. Can you feel it?"

He shoves my fingers against my breast to feel for myself.

"—Oh yeah. It doesn't hurt so I didn't notice it."

This all happened fast. Really fast, like head-spinning fast. A whirlwind. A wasted day, really.

Today I am grateful for cysts because women get cysts all the time. I read about cysts on WebMD. They're all over the internet. They clear up with antibiotics in no time. Just an off-day. Nothing to lose sleep over. Maybe I will rip this page out and forget today ever happened.

In addition to cysts, I am also grateful for Dante and Pauli. They are excited about Italy, and I am dying to take them. They downloaded a language app to their phones and they've been talking to one another in Italian. They're butchering the accents, but they're trying. It's cute to watch. I could watch those two carry on all day. As June fifteenth approaches, the dream of touching down in Italy draws ever closer. I can't wait! I have no idea whether Charlie is excited about Italy—he's still not mentioned golfing in Cinque Terre. But then, rocks don't talk, do they?

Flowers don't talk either. I'm scheduled for a mammogram tomorrow, but I'm not going to tell Charlie about it. I'm not telling anyone. It's just a cyst, so there's nothing to tell. Women get cysts all the time.

Thursday, June 6th

Mammogram done. Biopsy report back. Lose my breast? That's like losing your name. You can't lose your name, it's yours. Mastectomy. Did I hear it right? Mastectomy happens to the lady down the street. It happens to bad women, women who deserve it. Maybe someone who hates her kids. A bad wife or a horrible daughter. Me? Sentenced to death. What did I do?

After that, I lost my bearings. Came home, went to bed. I just want to sleep. Wake up or not—it doesn't matter. I am grateful for nightmares, because when I wake up, this nightmare will be over. This is a nightmare.

Nightmares aren't real, Lily. Go back to sleep now. Everything is okay.

Friday, June 7th

Up early. I've got the flu. So I say. Another day at home. Where do I turn? I should pray, but what does God know about losing a breast? I don't remember the Virgin Mary losing her breast. Whatever I do, I won't let Dante and Pauli down. They're going to Italy and I'm going with them. I could tell my mom, but she will cry. What can Mom and Dad do, anyway? Here I am:

Alone.

I need Charlie more than puny words on a page can say. But I'm not ready to tell him. He's not ready to hear it either. I read a poem that said something like "Suffering is the fountain from which love flows." I'm not sure I get it, but I sure as hell hope it's true.

Saturday, June 8th

That little bastard is real. I can feel it growing in my breast. I hate it. Despise it. But I have to face it because my life is in my body. Charlie comes in my body. My boys came out of my body. Hell, you can't even go shopping without your body. I love my body, so why is my body trying to kill me? Sonofabitch.

Sunday, June 9th

What will I tell Charlie? Charlie loves my body even more than I do; he might shy away from saying he loves me, but that hard rock isn't shy about loving my body. He likes it just the way it is: with shapely, perky boobs. Will Charlie love me in sickness as well as in health? Or were those words he just carelessly read off a page? Is he going to walk out and go play golf when I say mastectomy? I'm not ready to find out. Not yet. Not ready to tell anyone.

Monday, June 10th

I met Dr. Murphy today. He looks too young to be a surgeon. Handsome, confident, pleasant, but business-like. He could be single. No ring on his finger, if that means anything these days. Perfect for Alexa.

Actually, I met with the entire team, as they call themselves. Representatives from surgery, nursing, radiology, chemotherapy, nutrition, physical therapy, and a couple of others I'm not sure about were assembled to entice me to believe in their treatments. They sat around an oblong table, politely planning gruesome acts that they view as kindness. The team is in a hurry—they laid out the schedule without consulting me first.

"June seventeenth is out of the question. I'm going to Italy June fifteenth."

A deadly silence falls over the room.

"That would be a mistake," says Dr. Murphy.

"How could going to Italy ever be a mistake?"

"Your tumor is contained. If we get at it quick, it's all in your favor."

"My family is going to Italy this Saturday and I am going with them."

Dr. Murphy picks up his phone, and a minute later, the big gun barrels through the door. Dr. McDowell takes my hand and leads me to a small consultation room that appears to be designed for troublemakers like me. We sit on two tiny chairs, and he puts his face directly in front of mine, only six inches away, and looks me in my eyes:

"Lily, if you insist on going to Italy, we won't stop you. But please don't. I don't want to lose you. Your odds are good right now, but don't gamble with your life. Cancer changes everything, but Italy will still be there next year. I want to be your doctor for a long time. Please."

That was it. I can't argue with someone who cares about me like that. So Italy is cancelled or postponed or something—for me at least. Who knows what Charlie will do about Italy, school runs, not-so-perky breasts, or anything else. I guess it's time to find out.

Tuesday, June 11th

I hid in my room yesterday afternoon and cried like a baby. For hours. Why am I by myself? Why do I feel alone? So I sat Charlie down last night for "the talk," and I knew right away why I'm handling all this alone: because I am alone. All I saw with Charlie were red flags. Charlie says he didn't sign up for cancer, but he will try. He'll give it his best. Apparently, mastectomy, chemotherapy and hair loss weren't on his radar, either. He doesn't know what to say about that. He'll have to think about it, he says, but he promises to give it some thought. Never mind the fact that I have to think about it every minute of every day now. I have no choice.

Apparently, Charlie does.

I told him, "Charlie, you have to grow up. You have

to give. You have to believe. We will get through this—together." Of course, me having to say this is a red flag in itself. He should be the one saying it. Not me. I'm embarrassed to write this. It's not pleasant or polite for a wife to say, but I'm not my mom: Charlie is useless.

Thursday, June 13th

Charlie and I are in a place we've never been before: I need him more than he needs me. For once, that puts him in the driver's seat. Mom and Dad agree to take care of Dante and Pauli, so I have no worries there, but they refuse to babysit Charlie. He will be running the show at Macklin Media. He has pirated Alexa out of Marketing to be his personal assistant, and she is probably just what he needs, someone to keep him organized. Dad and I believe he will do a good job managing the business—it's what he's good at. Besides, we don't really have a choice. He will do it his way, and all I can do is hope for the best. I'm out of gas—maybe for a while, maybe forever. I have to trust him to step up to the plate and hit the ball. All he has to do is hold the business together. I am counting on him—everyone is.

Saturday, June 15th

Today was a Day of Mourning in the Coscarelli household. At exactly 5:10 p.m. we observed one minute of silence as Flight 523—Atlanta to Milan took off —and we were not on it. It was the death of a dream. Like all grieving families, the feelings in the household ranged from frustration and anger, to disappointment and confusion, to consolation and acceptance. It was a solemn moment as our family came together to support and comfort one another. Condolences in the form of cards, calls, and flowers were sent from friends and family near and far. Rest in Peace, Italy.

That last paragraph is a fantasy. The truth is mundane. There were indeed a lot of mixed, conflicting feelings today—I'm certainly carrying a shitload of guilt for getting sick and disappointing my family. Charlie is happy to be taking control of Macklin Media, but he's pissed that he won't get to play golf at Cinque Terre. The boys are taking it the best; they're happy not to be stuck in museums learning about Leonardo DaVinci, Michelangelo, Julius Caesar, and the Holy Roman Empire. They are thanking God they didn't have to visit the Vatican. How ironic can it get?

The truth is, we don't really have words to express all these feelings. My family doesn't know how to communicate about anything deeper than sports, fake news, weather, Facebook, Instagram, and Twitter. In actuality, today I went to the pharmacy to pick up the medications needed for my surgery. Charlie used his extra day to get in a round of golf. Danny and Arianna took the boys and their cousins to the water park. In my family, the deepest we'll get about cancer or death is when my name comes up on the prayer list at church tomorrow. A few people will say they're going to pray for me. I hope they mean it.

Sunday, June 16th

Dr. McDowell says cancer changes everything, but that's not exactly it: staring at death changes everything. Before June sixth, I never thought about death—my own death that is. It's a dark topic. But life and death are pretty basic. I have to make up my mind. Do I want to live or die? I want to live. If I want to live, I have to give away my breast and do the treatments. If I want to live, I have to let the chips fall where they will with Charlie. I am starting to hate myself, and if loving Charlie makes me hate myself, something has to give. I'll wait and see, but I am beginning to suspect that Charlie and I will never be the same.

I'm putting my *Taste of Italy* journal away for a while. My surgery is tomorrow. Faith, hope, and love are all I have right now. I hope to survive. I have faith that Mom and Dad and Dante and Pauli love me, just as I love them. Charlie loves me in his own way. He's a rock, and I'm a flower, but I'm afraid that idea isn't working for me anymore.

I have come to grips with one thing. I was wrong; I am not my body. I need my body, but I am more than my body. I came into this world from my father's body and out of my mother's body, and I will leave this world when my body has its final say. But I entered this world with a flame in my heart. That flame is still burning. Whatever it is, or wherever it comes from, that flame propels me through life. It has travelled with me from the beginning. It is who I am, and by God, nobody is taking that flame away from me before it's my time to hand it off. Not if I have any say in it.

Italy, you will be there next year. But will I be there for you?

PRETTY IN WHITE

The Questions Begin

Around midnight, on the night Johanna was born, her parents, Katy and Terry, walked arm-in-arm down the hallway to the nursery of Lovejoy Medical Center to share the miracle of their new baby. They found Johanna wrapped in a white blanket, surrounded by a sea of other babies in shimmering pink and blue blankets.

This triggered a barrage of questions from the rattled new mother. "Why is Johanna wrapped in white? Did you run out of pink blankets? Can someone get her a pink blanket, please?"

"I called Doctor McDowell, and he will be here in the morning to explain this," the nurse told her.

Then Terry noticed that the pink and blue babies had their first and last names on their bassinettes, but Johanna's bassinette had only *Baby McFadden*. "Do you not know how to spell her first name? We spell it J-O-H-A-N-N-A, and it is pronounced Jo-Anna."

"Dr. McDowell is coming by to discuss this with you in the morning."

So Katy and Terry did the only thing they could do.

They went back to their room to wait for Dr. McDowell. In the middle of the night, the nurse jostled Katy out of a groggy post-partum daze to ask if she would like to breastfeed her baby.

"I'm ready if Johanna is," Katy replied.

So the nurse left and came back pushing a bassinette. In one fell swoop, she scooped out all eight pounds, two ounces of Baby McFadden, which she delivered to Katy's anticipating breast.

"It's such a sweet baby," said the nurse.

Katy was consumed with the glee and trepidation of breastfeeding her baby for the first time, so she didn't really pay attention. But Terry did, and when the nurse went out the door, Terry followed her down the hall.

"Why did you call our baby *it*?"

"Oh, I meant *her*," she said. Terry stared at the woman. After an awkward silence, the nurse said, "Dr. McDowell will be here in a couple of hours to discuss this with you." Then she shot down the hall and disappeared into the nurses' station.

Dr. McDowell arrived as promised. He stood before the seated parents, brow furrowed. "There is a concern. Johanna has a nicely formed vagina, but the nurses noticed that she has either an unusually large clitoris or a very small penis; they call it a micro-penis. The bottom line is that we're not sure whether Johanna is a boy or a girl."

Katy and Terry looked at one another. They had been telling everyone for months that their baby was a girl.

Dr. McDowell continued. "Most people have no

idea, but about one in fifteen-hundred babies are born with ambiguous genitalia. It's so common that there are neonatologists who specialize in figuring out what sex a baby is, could be, or should be. In Johanna's case, the condition isn't obvious, but the nurses did their job and spotted it. I recommend that we bring in a specialist."

So Dr. Pu, a neonatologist was called in, and after two tense days of genetic testing, ultrasounds, CT scans, and an MRI, Johanna was diagnosed with Congenital Adrenal Hyperplasia, CAH for short. Dr. Pu explained it this way: "CAH is a condition in which Johanna's adrenal gland doesn't produce cortisol, a hormone that combats stress and also plays a critical role in prenatal sex development. At one time, CAH was fatal; but with modern medical advances, CAH is rarely fatal if diagnosed at birth. So you can thank Dr. McDowell and the nurses for saving Johanna's life."

Dr. McDowell allowed himself a small smile and a nod. "Fortunately, Johanna should be able to live a long and healthy life with CAH, but she will need to take cortisone pills every day for the rest of her life. When she suffers physical or mental stress—a common cold, injury, or upsetting situation—she may need a cortisone injection. Also, Johanna will crave salt from time to time because her body doesn't absorb sodium efficiently, especially in high stress situations."

"That doesn't sound so bad," said Terry, his arms around Katy.

"There is more," Dr. McDowell continued. "Johanna has perfect XX chromosomes—she is as genetically female as Miss Universe or the girl next door—but since her adrenal gland didn't produce enough cortisol when she was developing into a female, she was over-exposed to male testosterone in your womb, Katy. So she has a slightly enlarged clitoris, an abnormally small uterus, and underdeveloped ovaries."

"You see," said Dr. Pu, "nature didn't finish the job of making Johanna into a perfect female, but we can help her out with surgery. I strongly recommend that we remove her uterus and ovaries because they could easily become cancerous in the future. I also recommend cosmetic surgery to trim the clitoris: we'll make it smaller to make her vagina look more feminine. These procedures aren't medically necessary—they're cosmetic, strictly for looks— but society can be cruel when a child doesn't fit into a neat category of boy or girl. Mr. and Mrs. McFadden, you wouldn't want Johanna to feel ashamed of how she looks down there, would you?"

At this point, Katy burst into tears. "So what are you saying?"

"We need your permission to proceed with the surgery," said Dr. Pu.

A bit jostled, Terry turned to Dr. McDowell, who frowned. "The appearance of Johanna's vagina is a concern, but it's only a problem if you make it a problem. It's her vagina. Why don't you wait and let her decide when she gets older? At some point, she can decide whether she wants cosmetic surgery or not. I recommend a wait-and-see attitude with her uterus and ovaries too. It's unlikely, but it is possible that her ovaries and uterus will continue to develop if left alone. It would be a miracle if they do, because then Johanna might be able to get pregnant and carry a baby someday."

That was enough for Katy and Terry, and with total trust in Dr. McDowell, they said no to the surgery. The next day they proudly carried Johanna home in a pink blanket, and made up their minds to love Johanna the way she was. It was quiet on the car ride home, but finally Katy said, "How can we be sure we made the right decision?"

"I agree with Dr. McDowell. This is our baby, but it's not our decision to make. Someday she will have a mind of her own and she can decide for herself. In the meantime, we will love her the way she is and not make a big deal of it."

"But we have to tell her at some point."

"We'll tell her in good time. We won't keep secrets or push it under the rug. But we won't make a mountain out of a molehill either."

And that was that. But as Johanna went from infant to toddler and into young childhood, it turned out that there was little to talk about. Except for the daily cortisone pills, an occasional salt craving, and a cortisone injection once in a blue moon, Johanna had a medically uneventful childhood. She grew up a healthy, happy girl, no different from any of the other girls in her circle—a little on the boyish side maybe, and good at math and football.

The Red Sea Debacle

By the time Johanna was fourteen, most of the girls at Lovejoy Middle School had gotten their period. But not her. She wasn't growing breasts either. The Queen Bees had nicknamed her "Flatty McFaddie," and she spent more time rough-housing with the boys than worrying about which one would ask her to prom. The pressure was on at school. Things were getting tense at home, too, as Johanna started asking questions for which there were no good answers.

Whatever Johanna's question, Terry's standard answer was, "Don't be too self-conscious." Katy, on the other hand, was losing sleep as month after month went by and Johanna still had no period. One afternoon, Katy knocked on Johanna's door.

"Can I come in?"

Katy closed the door behind her and perched on the side of her daughter's bed. It was to be the first of many talks about what they would come to call their "reproductive hopes."

"I'm hoping that somehow your ovaries will sprout some eggs and your uterus will grow so you can have a baby," Katy explained to her daughter. "Do you ever feel anything in your lower abdomen?"

"Like what?"

"Like tension? Cramps? Like it's sensitive or tingly down there?"

"I never feel anything down there."

So this first talk about reproductive hopes turned out to be about hope sinking. But hope was all they had. So Katy and Johanna vowed that if it was mind versus matter, mind was going to win, no matter what.

"I'm not giving up hope," Katy reassured Johanna.

"Me, neither," Johanna promised.

Every morning, kneeling on her bedroom carpet, Johanna would whisper, "Dear God, please make my ovaries work, and I promise to glorify you every time I have a period."

Katy was into new-age spirituality, and every morning, noon, and night she would visualize a bloody red lining and would launch her vision into the universe with the words, "Creator of All Life, deliver this bloody lining to my little girl's uterus."

Three months went by while Katy and Johanna prayed to God and begged the universe. Then, on the afternoon before her fifteenth birthday, crazy-happy Johanna barged through the front door. "Mom!" she yelled, "it's here! I got my period!" The heavens had let loose. Johanna's panties were red and messy and beautiful. Katy came rushing down the stairs and hugged her daughter. They jumped for joy and thanked God. Later that afternoon, Johanna unwrapped the most amazing birthday gift her mother ever gave her—a box of tampons. Johanna loved unwrapping that box. It was funny. It was awesome.

And too good to be true.

Ten days went by and Johanna was still bleeding. Two weeks and still no end. Something wasn't right. Katy called Dr. McDowell. More blood tests, another ultrasound and MRI.

Dr. McDowell looked tired. "I'm afraid that what we're seeing isn't a menstrual period," he said. "It's blood seeping from your uterus and ovaries. It's the worst case scenario; your uterus and ovaries are diseased and dangerously pre-cancerous. It's time to face reality. We have to take steps."

One month after her fifteenth birthday, Johanna checked into Lovejoy Medical, where the surgeon removed her uterus and ovaries. Katy had dared to hope—but there are times when a mom is just a mom, and her hopes for her daughter don't change a thing.

A Routine Visit to the Doctor

Almost fifteen years have passed since the Red Sea debacle, and with her thirtieth birthday on the horizon, Johanna is sitting in Dr. McDowell's waiting room, ready to endure the ultrasound necessary for Dr. McDowell to renew her annual prescription for estrogen.

Johanna resents coming to the office for this. For one thing, the office is right across the street from Babies R Us, and the reading rack is full of parenting and pregnancy magazines. On top of that, there's always at least one mother-to-be jabbering on about her pregnancy. Today is no exception, and Johanna's the only other person there to take the brunt.

"I'm pregnant; it's my first," announces the jabberer.

Johanna manages a polite smile and mumbles, "Congratulations."

"I'm not that far along so I'm not showing yet. I don't think so, anyway."

Johanna glances up and right back down. "Nope."

"Are you pregnant?"

That's it. Johanna blows her off with the evil eye and moves over a couple of seats.

But the jabberer continues. "I'm only asking because I didn't think I'd get pregnant. All I can say is take your pill every day. I mean every day. I haven't told the father yet. I hope he's on board. He has money, so he should be good for child support. But basically, I may be on my own with this child. I'm committed to being a good parent though."

Johanna quietly wonders if this woman has ever heard the word *overshare.*

"How long have you been a patient of Dr. McDowell? This is my first time here, but my sister has been Dr. McDowell's nurse for eight years and she worships the guy. If you've been here before, maybe you know her. Her name is Maria."

Johanna returns a blank stare.

"My boss highly recommends Dr. McDowell. Says he saved her life."

Johanna could say the same, but she's not about to go into that; she isn't going to say anything, not even "Shut up" because that would be giving this woman just the attention she's looking for. Instead, Johanna stares straight ahead and tries to keep the sadness at bay. *This woman has no clue how lucky she is. I would give anything to become a mother.* Johanna is inside herself pretty deep when the examination room door opens and a nurse's voice rings out.

"Alexa Arioli?"

The jabberer jumps up. "Nice to talk to you. Tell my

sister hey if you see her back there—her name is Maria, remember."

It's too late for Johanna, though. This waiting room is more than she can handle. She feels dizzy and holds on to the chair to keep from toppling to the floor. She digs through her purse and pulls out a cortisone pill, but she has no water to wash it down. To hell with the water; she swallows it dry and is about to puke when the door opens again.

"Johanna McFadden?" Just in the nick of time. "How are you today?"

"I'll be fine once I get this over with."

"You know, that was my sister you were sitting with."

"She told me. An open book, I'd say."

"That's putting it nicely," says Maria.

Johanna concentrates on her balance and steps on the scale. She's put on a few pounds, but weight gains are common when you live in a body that gets estrogen from a patch. Johanna studies the diagrams on the wall, images of body parts that she doesn't have and doesn't relate to. Where other women see images of a uterus, ovaries, and fallopian tubes, Johanna sees a cattle skull with tulips dangling from the horns.

Maria has checked Johanna in and out of this office so many times that she should understand by now that Johanna is not like the other women who come here. Maria pulls out a hand-held device with Johanna's medical records. "We need to update your chart. When did you have your last period?"

"Why are you asking me that?" Johanna rails back in disbelief.

"We have to update your chart."

"I don't have periods. You know that. Don't make me explain it to you."

Maria drops the device to the floor. "Oh my God, I forgot you had a hysterectomy. What was I thinking?" She scrambles down to grab the device.

"Can we get this over with?" pleads Johanna.

Maria leads Johanna down the hall to the ultrasound room, and, as they enter, announces, "It's here."

Johanna stops dead in her tracks. "Did you just say *it* is here?"

"I just meant her three o'clock appointment is here, that's all." Maria backs out the door, and rushes down the hallway.

The ultrasound tech hands Johanna a white wrap, and says, "The gown opens in the front." She steps outside while Johanna undresses, and after re-entering, she instructs Johanna to lie back and bare her lower abdomen. She smears goo below Johanna's belly-button and glides the wand methodically from top to bottom and side to side. "What are we looking for? A boy or girl?"

"Just get this over with," groans Johanna.

The technician continues to study the image. "It looks like there could be twins, maybe one of each."

"For God's sake, did you read my chart?"

The tech pulls off her glove, scrolls through the chart, and goes bug-eyed. "My mistake. That must be your colon

I was seeing. Sometimes when the colon loops, it looks like a fetus. I'm sorry. I don't see anything to worry about. Get dressed, and I'll make sure Dr. McDowell has the report by tomorrow morning."

The Stranger

Johanna is accustomed to misunderstandings—she has lived with them all her life. She keeps her dignity by assuring herself that she's never the one who creates the misunderstandings; they're caused because people make the wrong assumptions about her. And they usually say they're sorry.

Their assumptions have real consequences, though. Johanna is about to turn thirty, and she has never shared a romantic kiss with anyone—ever. The idea of intimacy terrifies her. In middle school, when other girls were learning to flirt, Johanna was learning to rely only upon herself. In high school, she threw herself into her studies, and by the time she got to college, Johanna was no longer sure what she was avoiding. It was as if a switch turned off when she was fifteen, and now she's forgotten where the switch is. A dull and unmoving shame seems to have set up shop in her lower stomach, and Johanna is sure she'll be a cat lady the rest of her life.

As Johanna exits Dr. McDowell's office, a stranger follows her into the elevator. Johanna swallows. It's just the two of them. She steps to the rear for the ride to the ground floor. Out of the blue, this unknown man breaks elevator etiquette and asks a question he should not be asking:

"So how's your health?"

Okay, it's one thing when a crazy woman asks personal questions in a waiting room, but it's another when a perfect stranger invades your privacy in a confined space. Johanna tenses up and stares straight ahead, but the man keeps talking.

"I'm sorry; I know I'm being rude. What I mean is, I saw you come out of Dr. McDowell's office, and you appear very healthy to me. Really fit, actually. You probably have a boyfriend or a husband, or at least you'll say you do; why wouldn't you? Look, I would like to meet you— if there is any way two strangers can meet under these circumstances." Having made his pitch, the stranger stands quietly.

Johanna fumbles through her purse for her cell phone, and tries to remember if this kind of stranger invasion was covered in her self-defense class.

When the elevator door opens, she delivers a searing glare and storms into the lobby, which she is relieved to see is full of people. Key in hand, she makes a beeline to her car, gets in, locks the door, and pushes the ignition. As she backs out, she looks over her shoulder. The stranger is opening the car next to hers, and he seems as startled to see her as she is to see him. He shrugs his shoulders in a bewildered boyish apology, flashes an innocent smile, and caps it off with a little wave. Johanna slams on the brake and sits there, her car rocking back and forth like an amusement park ride.

Instead of getting in his car, the stranger stands and

stares at Johanna through her car window. Johanna is half in and half out of the parking space. She has to choose— back out and drive away or roll down the window and say something. She cracks the window, just an inch, and barks, "What kind of question was that?"

"Sorry to scare you. When I saw you in the elevator, I couldn't help myself. I couldn't let you get away without saying something, even if what came out of my mouth was stupid. My name is Brendan."

"Well, it was stupid. And the state of my health is none of your business. Why should I talk to you, anyway?"

"You probably shouldn't. And if you were my sister, I would tell you to get out of here. Fortunately, you aren't my sister, and I hope you will at least take my number and contact me if you want. Of course, I would understand if you don't."

Johanna swallows and tries to stop her hands trembling. Is Brendan even his real name? If he is being honest (and if he wasn't released from prison this morning, which he could have been, for all she knows), what does he want? At this moment, Johanna feels a crack in her protective armor. It's a small concession deep inside her, but she feels something move that has never moved before. She tells Brendan nothing about herself, not even her name—but as he rattles off his number, she slams it into her contact list.

Then she drives away.

She thinks about what just happened. In fact, she thinks of nothing else for the next three days. She dwells on it to such an extent that she has to give herself a cortisone shot to deal with the stress. For Johanna, the idea of contacting Brendan is like getting on board a plane you know is going to crash.

This is when armed-and-protected, soon-to-be-thirty, career-oriented, mind-of-her-own, I-don't-listen-to-anybody, cat-lady-forever Johanna turns to her mother. If anyone understands Johanna's torment, it's Katy. Katy has lived with it for three decades, and all she wants is to see her daughter happy. So Johanna spills it all.

"Look, Mom, I can't contact him. When would I tell him about my condition? Should I bring it up in the popcorn line at the cinema? 'Hey, I'll take a Coke, and just thought I should mention that when I was born, the doctors weren't sure if I was a boy or a girl.' Maybe I could lead him on and wait until we're ready for our first kiss. That's it. I'll stare into his gorgeous, green eyes and whisper, 'Did I mention that I have some pretty mixed-up genitalia?'"

"Maybe it would be best not to say anything for a while," her mother counsels. "Warm up to him first; see if he likes you and if you like him. Relax and enjoy it for whatever it turns out to be." This sounds like her dad's standard advice—"Don't be too self-conscious"—and Johanna has never understood that idea.

"Suppose he does like me? Then what? Hit him with, 'Nice to know you, but don't get too interested, I can't have children?'"

"Questions have a way of finding their own answers,"

says Katy. "Let things work themselves out over time. Just remember to keep your dignity; the misunderstandings won't come from you, they'll come from the expectations Brendan might have of you. And expectations can change."

"That's easy for you to say, Mom, but we both know I'm as mixed up as a Rubik's Cube." She laughs bitterly.

Johanna is a "get it over with" kind of girl. Later that day, she sends Brendan a text:

Johanna here, met you at medical center. How r u?

She doesn't expect a reply; it's probably a phony number and, even if it is real, he'll have forgotten her—it has been five days after all. He probably plays this game with women all the time.

Shock of shocks. Brendan replies.

Good to hear from you. Am fine. u?

It dawns on Johanna that she'll be telling the truth if she says that she's fine too. She replies the same.

Brendan wastes no time.

Meet for coffee tonight?

If Johanna thinks about it for too long, she is going to come up with an excuse to say no. So she holds her breath.

Yes

Coffee Bean @ 8?

All systems are go. Johanna is about to turn thirty, and she's giving herself an awesome birthday gift: she's going on her first date! Sort of.

The second Johanna closes her phone, memories of the Red Sea Debacle begin to flood her mind. Hope and despair go to war inside her. Hope shouts, "You are who you are and anyone who doesn't love you as you are doesn't deserve you!" In response, despair asks, "Who would possibly want you?"

Johanna decides there is only one way to handle this: She is going to ignore her mother's advice to go slow. She is going to shove who she is in Brendan's face right at the get-go and watch him squirm as he makes up excuses to run for the door. She heads to the Coffee Bean Café to put the screws to this guy who had the audacity to hit on her when she was trapped in an elevator.

When she arrives, Brendan is sitting in the corner. Johanna gives him enough eye contact to let him know she is there, but offers nothing more, not even a hello. She wants him to know—before he even gets the chance—that she cannot, and will not, be hurt. *Not by him. Not by anyone.* She goes straight to the barista and orders an iced mocha latte. Drink in hand, she approaches Brendan, who rises to greet her. She sits down across from him and, before there's a chance for any small talk, before they even exchange hellos, Johanna begins a litany on who she is.

"I'm just going to put this out there, so there won't be any confusion. When I was born, nobody knew if I was a boy or a girl. . ."

And she proceeds to lay out the entire story of her life with CAH—including her ambiguous genitalia, cortisone shots, and why she thinks this meetup doesn't have a snowball's chance in hell. After fifteen minutes of sharing too much information, Johanna wraps it up with, "So now you know what you are getting yourself into. If I am repulsive to you, please go, because I can't do anything about it."

Through this entire barrage, Brendan has listened attentively. And when she finishes, he looks across the table and calmly says, "Interesting. Do you crave salt or do you have that under control?"

Johanna flinches and stares. Where any other man would have been squirming and gasping, Brendan has shown no visceral reaction whatsoever. She hasn't ruffled a single feather. Moreover, she hasn't said a word about craving salt—it's the one thing she left out.

"How do you know about salt craving?"

"I studied CAH in med school. I know the textbook basics, but I've never had a patient with CAH or known anyone with it; you're the first. What you described sounds exactly like what I studied. So do you have salt cravings?"

"Not usually. That's one thing I do have under control." She takes her attitude down a notch and nervously shifts in her chair. "Sorry. I don't talk to many people about my condition, and I've never met anyone who actually knew anything about it. I guess you're a first for me."

"I'm not an expert on CAH, but I'd like to learn more about it. I mean, I'd like to learn more about you, if that's okay."

"So, you're a doctor?"

"Yes, I'm a trauma surgeon, so sometimes I'm in the regular surgery unit and at other times I'm in the Emergency Room. My goal is to be able to conduct major surgery in any makeshift space—on battlefields, in villages ravaged by natural disasters, on the freeway if necessary. It's an up-and-coming specialization, what with all the military casualties and terrorist attacks these days."

"So you understand that I can't have a baby, right? I'd like to adopt someday, but I cannot have a baby. You need to know that."

Brendan, being more experienced in the rules of hook ups and romance, deflects this for a later time, if that time ever comes. "Maybe we can talk about children some other time—after the first date perhaps! But yes, I understand your situation."

A Natural Woman

The evening turns out to be a success. Johanna is amazed by how much fun she's having. Brendan must be one of the warmest, kindest, and most fascinating individuals she has ever known—the kind of guy she could really get into. In one life-changing hour on a Tuesday night, this stranger has helped Johanna finally understand Aretha Franklin's eternal words: *You make me feel like a natural woman.*

The chemistry is there. She and Brendan both like travel and adventure. They share similar spiritual beliefs. Their families are alike. Brendan has finished his residency and Johanna is a marketing executive with a bright future. The timing is perfect for a serious relationship—so perfect that Johanna asks Brendan for a special gift on her thirtieth birthday. As the two of them stroll along the wooden deck overlooking a secluded pond behind Johanna's parents' house, the soft summer moon rising to the rhythm of katydid chatter, Brendan wraps his arms around Johanna's waist, pulls her close, and gives her a passionate kiss. Her first ever. It's so powerful that Johanna's heart goes into arrhythmia. Her breathing accelerates. Her body shivers. This is the kind of stress reaction Johanna is supposed to avoid, and she wonders whether she should rush inside and take an extra cortisone pill before she passes out. Then it hits her. This is good stress—the kind you don't take a pill to get rid of. The kind you feel when you're falling in love. "To hell with cortisone pills," she says as she pushes herself into Brendan. And the two of them melt together under the wide and sultry moon.

The expression "Time flies when you're having fun" was coined for Brendan and Johanna. The next year flies by, peppered with many falling-in-love firsts: first road trip, first dinner guests, first dog rescue, and first Fourth of July fireworks. It's all juicy, and before long, Johanna and Brendan are on the conveyor belt to marriage. The conveyor belt is like the check out in the grocery store; your items sit there doing nothing, moving gradually onward. Before long, Katy wants to know, "When are you two making it official?" Terry is asking, "Is Brendan ever going to pop the question?"

Next thing you know, Brendan finds himself doing something he has never done; he is down on one knee asking Johanna a question that will change them both forever. Soon, Terry is inundated with bills for the wedding, and Johanna and Brendan are riding in a horse-drawn carriage; marching down the aisle to a string quartet; basking in the pungent perfume of flowers; and swearing before God, family and friends. Father Miles Joyce pronounces the blessing: "May you love one another as long as you live and live forever in the love of God" He presents Dr. and Mrs. Brendan Murphy to the wedding guests, and all this makes a dozen women, three hormonal girls, and one financially challenged father cry their eyes out. Some dreams do come true.

Your Mistake Has a Name

It has been two years since Johanna and Brendan got back from their honeymoon in Cabo. They are living their dreams. In fact, they have decided to take their dreams to the next level: they are ready to adopt a child. They have done their homework on how to adopt and are working with an agency that will help them search for that one special child destined to be with them. They would love to adopt a healthy newborn, but they know that can take years. Plan B includes other children who may need them—a child who is older or disabled.

The fact that Johanna and Brendan are educated, financially well-off, and have a nice home puts them in good stead with expectant mothers studying family profiles. It's hard to say how Johanna's condition will affect the adoption process—it could work in her favor if an expectant mother feels sympathetic to the fact that Johanna will never be able to give birth to a child of her own, or work against her if an expectant mother errantly believes that CAH is contagious or that it will limit

Johanna's ability to be a good parent. Johanna has doubled down on the lesson she learned when she met Brendan: full disclosure is the best policy. Put it all on the table has become a core belief for her. Get things out in the open, and there won't be any confusion later on.

Johanna and Brendan have learned the rigors of adoption; it's not for the meek or dabblers. The questionnaires are endless; there are family histories, criminal background checks, credit checks, health histories, education and employment histories, psychological reports, and reference letters. Every nook and cranny of their home has been inspected and photographed, from the attic to the darkest recesses of the basement. They have supplied proof that there is no lead in the paint on the walls and no poisons under the sink. As directed, they installed a fence around the pool and purchased a gun safe for the twenty-two caliber that Brendan hasn't shot in fifteen years. Dr. McDowell submitted a letter stating that Johanna's condition will not affect her performance as a parent, and that, in his opinion, she isn't likely to die from natural causes in the next twenty years! Social workers have interviewed their neighbors, friends, and co-workers to find out what kind of people they are, looking for any stray shred of information that might suggest they won't be fit parents.

Johanna has found the process comforting; every hurdle passed, and no stone left unturned, means that she and Brendan are ready to be parents. They have reached the end of their home study, the final stage before their names go on the adoption registry, and they can start looking for the child they are meant to find. Johanna gets an email from Arianna Coscarelli, the social worker assigned to their case. Arianna wants to meet with Johanna and Brendan as soon as possible—this afternoon or tomorrow morning at the latest. Johanna texts Brendan. He has a sick patient to admit to the hospital, the waiting room is backed up, and there is no way he can get away. Johanna will have to meet with Ms. Coscarelli alone. As she drives to the adoption agency, Johanna's mind is fully focused on the *why* of the meeting. What news does Arianna have for her? It would be unusual, but given her run of good luck since she met Brendan, maybe Arianna has already found the right baby for them. It's a crazy thought, but maybe this is the day!

When she arrives, Johanna is quickly escorted into Ms. Coscarelli's office. Johanna has grown fond of Arianna over the last three months; she likes to think that their bond is almost sisterly. It is 4:15—she is marking the moment, hoping that this is the big day. Arianna closes the door, sits down behind the desk, and leans forward. Johanna slides to the edge of her seat and leans toward Arianna, ready to receive the gift that the universe is about to deliver.

"Johanna, there is a problem with your application. Why didn't you tell us that Brendan has a child? That's a problem."

"What kind of question is that?" rebuffs Johanna, pulling away and sitting up straight.

"On your application. You didn't say that Brendan already has a child."

"Of course I didn't. We don't have a child. I'm not able to have children. You know that." Johanna's voice is loud and clipped.

"I do know that. But we discovered that Brendan has a little boy named Cody who is three years old. The little boy lives with his mother; I've talked with the mother personally. Do you mean to tell me you didn't know that, Johanna?"

"That's impossible! I would know that if it were true. But it's not. Brendan doesn't have a little boy named Cody. There's a mix-up. Somebody is lying or something. What would make you think that Brendan is this boy's father?"

"According to the boy's mother, Brendan has been paying her child support since he found out she was pregnant, over three years ago."

"I don't know that and neither do you! There is some misunderstanding here." Her heart races out of control; she's breathing heavy and sweating profusely.

"According to Cody's mother, Brendan pays his child support like clock-work. That's a plus as far as your application goes. But he has absolutely zero contact with the boy—that's a negative—it calls into question what kind of father he is going to be."

Johanna keels over, holding back from hurling her lunch. Arianna hands her a box of tissues and goes to get a glass of water. When she returns, Johanna is putting on her coat.

"Listen, Johanna. Officially, your application is still in the home study phase. That buys you some time to straighten this out. But you have to get it worked out before we can move forward, and that is presuming we *will* move forward, which is far from guaranteed. Why don't you talk to Brendan and let me know if you want to withdraw your application."

"Withdraw our application?" Johanna gasps.

"If we reject your application, you may never be able to adopt. It would be better to withdraw your application before it gets rejected, so there's no official record of this. I'm not telling you what to do, but you might have better prospects if you weren't married to Brendan. You should probably see a lawyer. If you don't have one, my husband is Danny Coscarelli—here's his card. Don't be afraid to call him. You have two months to get your ducks in a row. After that, we make a decision." And with that, Arianna shows Johanna out the back door.

Johanna's tears keep coming. The streets weave in front of her. She accelerates when she should slow down and slows down when she ought to speed up. It's a miracle she makes it home. She doesn't even try to park in the garage out of fear she would pile into Brendan's car. She marches into the kitchen, grabs a bottle of water, and pops a cortisone pill. *Better take two.* She needs a cortisone injection, but she doesn't trust herself to administer it.

Brendan saunters into the kitchen to find Johanna with her head cocked back, pouring salt down her throat. He approaches to take the salt shaker out of her hand, but she spins around, screams, "Don't touch me!" and keeps pouring.

"What's going on?" he asks.

"I found out about Cody from Ms. Coscarelli this afternoon."

Time stops. Brendan looks out the window for far too long, then says, "I've been meaning to talk to you about that."

"Meaning to talk to me. How long have you been meaning to talk to me about this, Brendan? Three years? I'm dying to hear what else you've been meaning to talk to me about. Any more kids I don't know about? Prostitutes? A mistress or two?"

"Nothing else. Just Cody."

Johanna downs another mouthful of salt.

"I've wanted to tell you since I found out about it," explains Brendan.

"*It?*" bellows Johanna. "Are you calling your child *it?*"

"I mean *him*—Cody. I met a girl at a party a few weeks before I met you. She came on to me real hard, and I went with it. It was a hook up; she and I never dated. She wasn't my type. Later she contacted me and told me she was pregnant. In the meantime, I met you. I knew you were the woman of my dreams, and I didn't want to lose you, so I figured I'd keep it to myself until the time was right. Soon you and I were engaged, then married, and I still hadn't told you. I was trapped in a lie. I didn't want to hurt you."

"You didn't want to hurt me. And you didn't think this would hurt me? Making me a fool in front of my family? Squashing my dreams in front of the world?"

"It was a mistake, Johanna."

"Stop calling your child *it*. Your mistake has a name!"

Johanna turns away from Brendan and sinks into a chair at the kitchen table.

"I'm never going to get a baby now. Leave me alone."

Brendan wants to comfort her, but he can't. He goes to the living room to sit alone and stare out the window while Johanna sobs in the kitchen. After a few minutes, Johanna throws some clothes and cosmetics in a bag and heads to her parents' house. Her mother will give her a cortisone shot. Her father will say nothing. That's all she needs right now.

Rock, Paper, Scissors

Living with CAH, Johanna has learned how to harden in the face of adversity. Her survival has depended on it. The next morning, she gets to her office bright and early. Nothing has changed there; she can always count on her job to pull her through. She will throw herself into work. She will take on a new project and go for a promotion. She needs to find a place to live. Cancel the bank cards. Change the insurance policies.

Brendan lied. He humiliated her. She wants out, and she's not wasting any time. That afternoon, Johanna blindly follows an unassuming lady in a plain blue dress into the waiting room of Mr. Danny Coscarelli, *attorney extraordinaire*. The room is high-end traditional: elegant fabric, solid wood, and rich colors on the walls. Tea and cookies are lined up in perfect order on the sterling silver serving tray. A larger-than-life portrait of Mr. Coscarelli towers above the fireplace. The room whispers "Trust Mr. Coscarelli" to those whose lives are tearing apart at the seams.

Mr. Coscarelli listens attentively to Johanna's tragic story, and then surprises her with an idea she hadn't considered. "You don't want a divorce—you want an annulment. An annulment doesn't mean you were married and split up; it means you were never married in the first place. The grounds are there. This man withheld critical information that would have impacted your decision to marry him in the first place. The marriage smells of fraud. If you had known the truth about this child, would you have married this man?"

But before Johanna can even think about it, he answers his own question. "Of course not. That's why he didn't tell you. The man is a deceiver. A swindler. You'll never know what you would have done because he didn't give you a chance to decide for yourself."

Johanna sits and listens. If anyone had attacked Brendan like this a mere twenty-four hours ago, Johanna would have defended him to the death. Now she says nothing.

Mr. Coscarelli is prepared to file the annulment papers as soon as Johanna gives the go ahead. "Go home and sleep on it, and call me tomorrow morning. Most importantly, stay away from Brendan. You can't trust anything that comes out of his mouth. After the annulment, everything will go back to the way it was before you met him. All traces of Brendan Murphy will vanish."

Johanna tries to go back to work, but ends up sitting on a park bench, staring into space. All traces of Brendan will vanish? She can't imagine. She's not the hardliner she was before she met Brendan; he has changed that. And the more she thinks about it, the more confused she gets.

That evening, Johanna invites her mother to meet her for dinner. Johanna's stomach is a bubbling cauldron. She's not hungry, but maybe she can keep a bowl of soup and some crackers down.

As soon as they sit down, Katy asks, "What are you going to do?"

"I'm getting an annulment. What else can I do? He has ruined my life."

Katy scrunches her forehead. "How has he ruined your life?"

"You're taking his side?"

"It's not about sides. It's about you. Brendan is the best thing that ever happened to you, and you're giving up that easy? Listen to yourself."

"Listen to what? I have every right. Nobody's going to blame me for this."

"Don't make yourself out to be a victim. Brendan didn't do this to you. He did it to himself. He did it because he didn't want to hurt you. Think about what you're doing before you go off half-cocked."

"So you really are taking his side." Johanna spits out her words and her face turns red.

"Okay. Brendan made a mistake—a bad one—he screwed up royally. But you're the one holding the cards. Why not take a bad situation and make it better? Why can't you forgive him?"

"Forgive him? I am not giving in to this shit."

"You wouldn't be giving in. All you would be giving up are your expectations. You expected Brendan to be perfect. He isn't. You, of all people, should understand that part of the problem is your expectations."

"That's easy for you to say. You've never had to deal with a disappointment like this."

Those words punch Katy between the eyes. She stares across the table and bites her lip. Dr. McDowell's words are as relevant to her today as they were thirty-three years ago. . . *a concern is a problem only if you make it a problem.*

"You might be surprised to know the disappointments I've faced," is all she says.

"I can't eat anything," says Johanna, pushing her food to the side.

Katy picks at her food while Johanna plays rock-paper-scissors in her head. Brendan has cut her deep (scissors); she will smash him down (rock); and cover it all with the Petition for Annulment Mr. Coscarelli will file in court tomorrow (paper). Then, as her mom helplessly looks on, Johanna texts Brendan:

I've made a decision about our future.

Brendan replies immediately:

???

I'm coming over. Be ready.

With that, mother and daughter go their separate ways.

The Woman of My Dreams

One look at Brendan tells Johanna it has been a long twenty-four hours. His shirt is wrinkled, his hair a mess, his eyes dark and puffy. They sit down in the living room. Johanna says, "Let me get this straight. You met a girl at a party, took her home, had your fun, and knocked her up. Tell me something, Brendan. Do you have any kind of relationship with your little boy Cody?"

"I saw Cody right after he was born. I knew he was mine, and that's all I needed to know. His mother gets an automatic payment from my bank every month; that's the extent of it."

Johanna cringes. "You fathered a child, and the only relationship you have with him is an automatic payment. And you are claiming you did that for me? Do you really expect me to live with that guilt for the rest of my life, knowing you abandoned your son because of me?"

"I'm sorry for not telling you. I would have, eventually. I was ashamed and didn't want to face it—let alone drag you into it. I thought that after we adopted our own child it would be easier for you to accept. It's the biggest mistake of my life."

"Stop calling your son a mistake!" Johanna yells. "I would cut off my arm to have a child. You have a child, and you don't want him. How fucked up is that?"

"I know I've made a mess, but I don't want to lose you."

"It's not about me anymore. Or us. It's about Cody. You have more to offer this boy than an automatic payment. I'm setting you free to go and be a father. I won't respect you if you don't."

"What do you mean?"

"I'm getting our marriage annulled. I have a lawyer—Danny Coscarelli. I'm going to call him in the morning and tell him to file the papers. I want out of this mess. You were one big fat lie from the beginning. I should have known."

"Johanna, I was desperate. I didn't know what to do. When Alexa told me she was pregnant, I told her I had finally found the woman of my dreams and I couldn't let this come between you and me. I did it because I love you."

"It's too late," says Johanna. Then she freezes. "Wait. What did you say? Who's Alexa?"

"Alexa Aroli. Cody's mother. I told you. I met her at a party; I pay her child support. I don't know much about her, only that she works in movies and television. Her sister is a nurse in Dr. McDowell's office."

Johanna stares glassy-eyed, barely able to breathe. Then she scurries into the bedroom, throws a few things in a suitcase, and hurries out. No good-bye. No good luck. Just *get me the hell out of here.*

Brendan breaks down sobbing.

Once again, Johanna careens through the streets on her way back to her parents' house. She rummages under the seat for a salt shaker she stows away for moments like this, and, one hand on the wheel, sweeps around a corner, just as a man carrying a bulky trash bag steps to the curb. Johanna slams on the brakes and scares him so badly that he falls backward. Johanna jumps out and rushes over, only to realize that this is someone she has known all her life. Literally. It's Dr. McDowell. She takes his hand to help him back to his feet and he says, "Are you trying to kill someone who saved your life? Bad karma, Johanna."

And he laughs.

"I am so sorry. I'm a mess. I can't kill you—you know stuff about me nobody else knows. Besides, you're better for me than an entire shaker of salt!"

"Got some salt cravings going on, Johanna?"

"I could eat a brick of salt right now and it wouldn't do me a bit of good."

"Hmm. How's Brendan?"

"Talk about rubbing salt in the wound, Dr. McDowell."

"Well, I can take you inside and give you a cortisone shot if you're desperate."

"Thanks, Dr. McDowell. I'm sure I'll live. But you could answer a question for me."

"Is it serious?"

"As serious as it can get. I've wanted to ask you for a long time, but I chicken out because I'm afraid of what you would say. Now I have to ask."

"I'll give you the best answer I can, but I don't know everything."

"Dr. McDowell, I've had a confusing life, as you know, and right now, I don't know who I am or what I want. So can I ask: What did you think about me when I was born?"

His smile fades and he sighs. "You were a mystery to me. Back then, there were more questions than answers when it came to CAH. I was happy just to keep you alive, but I didn't know what life would have in store for you. In those days, everyone thought a baby with CAH was a mistake—a tragedy. I've learned a lot watching you grow up. I've watched you take the so-called tragic life you were given, and create something amazing. It has fulfilled me as a doctor watching you become strong and happy. I take a little credit, but I give a lot of credit to your parents, too. Parents are always heartbroken when they find out that their child isn't the perfect baby they were expecting; but your parents didn't cry or whine. They stood by you and loved you for who you were. I admire them for that, and wish I would have been more accepting of my own daughter."

"I love you, Dr. McDowell. Your daughter is lucky to have you as her father."

Dr. McDowell's brow flickers and he frowns. "I wish my daughter thought that. She's your age, but she hasn't talked to me for seven years. I love her and think about her every day. I guess she thinks I hurt her. I wasn't a perfect father—I made mistakes. But I made my mistakes out of love, not out of malice. Maybe I wasn't as understanding as I could have been. I would love to have her back in my life, but she doesn't respond to my calls, texts, cards, nothing. It's like I'm dead to her. My wife and I went to counseling; the counselor called it estrangement, and says it's more common than people think."

Johanna puts her hand on Dr. McDowell's shoulder. "That sounds terrible. I bet your daughter will get in touch with you someday—probably when she needs something. Kids expect their parents to be perfect and can't handle it when they aren't. She'll come back if you give her enough time."

Four Elbows Planted

When Johanna bursts through the front door, Katy immediately jumps all over her: "Did you tell Brendan about the annulment?"

Johanna waves her mom aside and asks a question of her own. "Where's Dad?"

"He's at the pond, waiting for the sun to set."

Johanna makes a beeline to the deck overlooking the pond, the place where she first kissed Brendan. Terry is leaning on the rail staring out over the water. Johanna quietly joins him, and they lean with four elbows planted on the rail, four eyes fixed on the sunlight reflecting off the pond. Finally, Terry breaks the silence. "Johanna, your mother and I support you no matter what you do. I don't want to meddle, but I want to give you my take on the situation. Over the years, I've learned that sometimes you get exactly what you want in life, but more often you get what you get—and then you figure out how to make the best of it. Take me, for example. I didn't know I wanted a baby with CAH until I had one. Once you came into our lives, you were the perfect child for me, and I wouldn't have traded you for any other baby. You made me whole. And I think your mother would say the same."

Johanna watches the final rays of sunlight cast deep shadows on her father's ruddy face, and feels loved. She hugs him and breathes his musty smell. "I know, Daddy." She turns and leaves her dad alone with the sunset. As she wanders into the house, the memory of Brendan's first kiss follows and crawls into bed with her. She lays her head on the pillow, and watches the rising moon dance at the window. She hears katydids chattering in the pines. She feels Brendan's hand in the small of her back pulling her into him. And as she drifts to sleep, Johanna knows she is not going to call Mr. Coscarelli in the morning.

Pizza It Is, My Bold Boy

It has been a year since Johanna left Brendan sobbing. It's Friday afternoon, and she is fixing a pizza in the kitchen. The doorbell rings. Johanna rinses her hands and skips to the door. A frazzled woman stands on the steps, with a little boy holding one hand and a suitcase in the other.

"Hi Johanna. Sorry, we're early. I hope it's not a problem."

Johanna opens the door to welcome the visitors in. "No worry, it's not a problem."

The three stand silently and suddenly the little boy asks, "Can I see the baby?"

"She's asleep, but you can have a look. We have to be real quiet so we don't wake her up." The two women and little boy tip-toe ever so quietly to a bedroom where a tiny newborn lies sleeping in a bassinette, wrapped in a glistening white blanket.

Johanna lifts the little boy up so he can see in the bassinette. "Can I kiss her?" he whispers.

"Yes, but be gentle." Cody plants a tender kiss on the baby's forehead.

"She's precious. Love the name. How did you come up with Sophia?" asks Alexa.

"Sophia means 'Wisdom.' It took a lot of wisdom to get

her here where she belongs, and I want to be reminded of that every day," smiles Johanna.

They quietly tip-toe back to the living room. "I may be late picking Cody up on Sunday, if that's okay. Believe it or not, I'm going on a spiritual retreat. I'll be hanging out with priests all weekend. I can't get into any trouble there. I hope." The two women laugh.

Alexa leaves and Johanna picks Cody up and holds him in her arms. "I'm happy I have a sister named Sophia," he tells her.

"I'm sure Sophia is happy to have a brother named Cody too. Your dad will be home in a few minutes. Let's put your suitcase away and get ready for dinner. Are you up for homemade pizza?"

"I love pizza!"

"Then pizza it is, my bold boy."

AN ADOPTION PROPOSAL

The following questions should be answered by the primary caregiver of the Waiting Family. Address your answers directly to the potential birth mother, who will consider your answers when deciding on the adoptive family.

Question 1. Describe yourself and the beliefs that guide you in making important decisions.

You probably expect me to paint a pretty picture of a perfect family, white picket fence and adoring husband, a beautiful house . . . well, sorry. I don't do phony; never have, never will. I believe in telling the truth as I know it, as best I can. You are facing one of the biggest decisions of your life, and if I were in your shoes, I would want the truth served straight, no mixers or fillers. So I am going to include the good, the bad and the ugly. This is about your baby—possibly *our* baby—and if we don't at least have honesty between us, what do we have?

One thing you should know is that I talk to myself. A lot. Pretty much non-stop. I may be driving, filling out a report, or pretending to pay attention in a meeting, but

I am most likely in my head, talking to myself, thinking about what I do and why I do it. If I had to describe myself in one sentence, I would say: Misfit geek who talks to herself.

I'm aware I might sound crazy here, but I don't think so. All I am saying is that I believe it's easy to do the wrong thing in most situations; doing the right thing usually takes awareness, reflection, and perseverance. I think about right and wrong, and try to do the right thing even when it is difficult or inconvenient. To me, life is about honesty and personal responsibility. Without it, we're all pretty much doomed.

Question 2: What is your biggest problem in life and how do you handle it?
I have a condition called congenital adrenal hyperplasia, CAH for short. You can Google it, but if I had to put it in a nutshell, I would say that CAH throws obstacles in my path that you probably don't even think about. My hormones occasionally go out of sync and, once in a blue moon, my body goes out of balance to the point where I have to take shots to control it. Nothing comes simple to me and I suppose it never will. So I have to plan ahead and keep my ducks in a row.

On top of this, doctors say I have ambiguous genitalia. I honestly don't know why doctors say that—they're not ambiguous to me. It has taken me a long time to speak out, but I think the ambiguity is in their heads, not in my genitalia. My body works well enough for me, and if I'm okay with it, why should anyone else care? If you care, you shouldn't. I can't get pregnant or give birth, but I am quite capable of being an awesome mother to your baby. That I promise.

If you met me, you would think I am a perfectly normal, healthy woman. I am actually quite attractive, and am hit on quite often by guys and girls alike. My condition isn't tattooed on my forehead. I may be a self-confessed geek but I don't look odd or unusual. Medically, however, I don't fit neatly into a box of boy or girl. Some doctors think everyone should fit in a box, but with the love and support of my primary care physician, my parents, and my husband, I have had the courage to push back against those who want me to undergo surgeries just to fit me in their boxes. When a person doesn't fit in your neat little box, wouldn't it be smart to get a different box? But of course, they don't think like that.

You wouldn't envy me for having CAH. Nobody would. But I wasted a good part of my life envying other women. It began in middle school when other girls started getting breasts and periods. I've never had a period in my life. In high school, I was jealous of girls with perfect bodies, which in my mind was every girl but me. I thought their bodies were perfect, even if they didn't. They had natural estrogen, lots of it, but I get my estrogen from the pharmacy up the street. It's a patch I wear every day—I have since I was fifteen.

Now in my thirties, I get queasy when I am around women who are showing off their cute babies, which again seems to be every woman but me. Don't take me wrong, I'm not blaming them. The problem is me, not them. I have an attitude. If you understand my condition, you know that I have no uterus or ovaries. I have no reproductive hopes. I try, but it's hard to be happy for them. Their joy is my despair.

I haven't always handled my attitude well. For over fifteen years, I built walls of protection to keep people out of my personal life. I made excuses for not dating or socializing, and when personal topics came up in conversations, I changed the subject. You probably won't relate to this, but until I was thirty, my mother knew every detail about my sex life. Which meant she knew nothing; there was nothing to know. Basically, I threw myself into my career, stayed at home and played with my cat. Back then, I didn't love myself, and I genuinely didn't believe that anyone except my parents could ever love me. So I made myself unlovable.

Three years ago, I realized that walling people out of my life amounted to nothing more than walling myself in. I was pretty damn lonely in that little closet I created. So since then, I have been taking down walls, one brick at a time. I have let go of the idea that life cheated me and learned to focus on the good that living with CAH has brought me. For one thing, CAH has taught me that feeling sorry for myself is a slippery slope, and if I succumb to self-pity for even one minute, I might get stuck there and never get back up. CAH has also taught me to think outside the box. I have to be flexible and creative—my mental and physical health depend on it. CAH is part of who I am, and growing up with it has made me strong. I believe there is virtually nothing—physical or emotional—that I cannot adapt to. When I am knocked down, I get back up. When I'm exhausted, I put one foot in front of the other. I forget what should have been and what used to be; instead I deal with what's going on right now and what's coming around the corner.

I used to think I was the only one who made myself unlovable. Now I know I'm not; lots of people do. True, few people have my exact same condition, but everyone has something that makes them feel self-conscious, tainted, or unlovable. Some may feel unlovable because of their slanted nose, chubby thighs, saggy breasts, big ass, or thin hair. Others may feel too tall, too short, too old, too stupid, or too shy. It could be their checkered past or lack of pedigree. At least my condition has a name.

Thankfully, I am living proof that there is plenty of love to go around if we open ourselves up to it. I couldn't have written that last sentence a few years ago, but love found me, and it changed everything.

Question 3: Who are the most important people in your life and why are they important?

To understand the important people in my life, you have to understand that a few decades ago, babies born with CAH did not typically survive. So I don't take life for granted; I've never had that luxury. It was only through the diligence of the nurses in the obstetrics and neonatology unit that I am still around to write this. To this day, I have deep feelings for the doctor who saved my life. He is an amazing man, and I love him like a father.

Even though I live a normal life, babies with so-called ambiguous genitalia are often viewed as mistakes. Freaks of nature. Rejects. Okay, everyone makes mistakes; we all slip and fall. But can you imagine what life is like when you *are* a mistake? It's your secret shame. And it never goes away—it's who you are and you can't change it.

Like all parents, my mom and dad were disappointed that their child was not perfect. They could have raised me as a mistake. They could have made a big deal out of my genitalia and turned my imperfections into an earth-shattering catastrophe. But they didn't. Instead, they gave me the gift of love and accepted me as I am. And for that, I will be indebted to them forever.

My walls of protection started coming down the day I met Brendan Murphy. He stirred me in ways I had never felt before. He accepted me as I am, and God knows, I love him for it. When I opened myself up to Brendan, I was finally able to say, "Hey, Great Big World, I am not a mistake. I am someone. I have a right to breathe the air. I have a reason to be alive. Someone besides my parents loves me."

That feeling was new to me. It was light and freeing—and absolutely terrifying. What if it was just a dream? And, in part, it was just a dream.

Brendan might be a doctor, but that doesn't mean he is smart when it comes to relationships. Two years into our marriage, I learned that Brendan had a secret himself, a secret past—a little boy that he fathered before we met, and who he conveniently forgot to tell me about. In fairness to Brendan, I believe he thought he was doing me a favor by not telling me. I know he didn't mean to hurt me, and he certainly didn't intend for me to find out the way I did. He was afraid to admit the truth to himself. I recognize all that and, knowing him, I believe he would think like that. Still, these are huge rationalizations and, by not telling me, he took away my freedom to decide for myself what to make of his little boy. Whatever his intentions, he was careless with my feelings and carefree with the truth. The whole thing was absurd because I would have loved him even more if he had come clean from the get-go.

Needless to say, we came very close to splitting up over this. The only thing that saved him was his sincere apology. He was truly remorseful—you could see it all over his face. People say that surgeons don't cry, but I know one who did.

Maybe I'm a fool for taking Brendan back. After all, he lied and maybe he'll do it again. But I don't think so. Throughout this ordeal, I spent a lot of time talking to myself. Through these inner conversations, I realized that while Brendan's imperfections are a concern, they aren't necessarily the problem I was making them out to be.

I faced up to a flaw in myself: Brendan made a mistake, but that doesn't mean he is a mistake. Here was a man who loved me, who gave my life meaning, and I was treating him like he was a mistake. Anyone can look back in time and see a dozen things they did but wish they hadn't, and a dozen things they didn't do, but wish they had. We're all guilty. Or maybe we're all innocent. You can make your own decision on that.

You might say I forgave Brendan, but I wouldn't put it that way. I was terribly disappointed in him, of course. But I believe in moving forward; dwelling on what he did wouldn't change the past. I didn't want to be stuck, spinning my wheels in the past. Besides, the word "forgive" sounds like I did a lot of giving, when in fact I did a lot of taking. I didn't give in. I didn't give up. I didn't let Brendan do whatever he wanted. I didn't act like nothing happened. Honestly, I don't see where I gave anything. I took the bull by the horns and told him he was going to be a good father if he wanted to be with me. I took control of the situation; it didn't take control of me.

To me, Brendan's most egregious error was that his son, now my step-son, was made to feel like a mistake. Which turns my thoughts to you, Potential Birth Mother. I know nothing about your situation, so I don't mean to presume, judge, or offend. We all know where babies come from. Perhaps your baby was conceived in love, maybe in lust, or in a less pleasant set of circumstances. I don't know what your baby means to you. I don't know what your baby means to the man with whom you conceived this child. Neither of us knows what meaning your baby will assign to her own life. But this I do know:

Your baby is not a mistake.

Given my history, I don't take life for granted. If it is

meant to be, here is what your baby will mean to me. Your baby will mean that I was born to love this child. My reason for getting out of bed in the morning will be to make sure your child feels valued and cared for. That she has a right to breathe the air. That she was born for a reason. We both know there is Plan B, and you don't have to give your baby the gift of life. You chose to do so. Unlike me, you have the privilege of giving life, and by that I mean giving life to me. Perhaps you will give me the opportunity to love your baby the same way my parents love me.

I will end by saying I am not a perfect person—far from it—but my hope, belief, and prayer is that I could be the perfect mother for your baby. I promise that this Waiting Family will love your child truly and deeply, albeit imperfectly, and that your child will never be a mistake.

THE TEXT MESSAGE

A Chocolate Donut

It's Wednesday morning, and Clare speeds through Lovejoy on her way to work. It's Donut Day at the office. Clare flies past Coffee Bean Café, and a text message pops up on her phone. It's from Alexa Arioli, the CEO's personal assistant:

Donuts! what kind do u want?

Clare grabs her phone, types *choc* and hits *Send* at the exact same moment the green Mini Cooper in front of her slows down to keep from hitting a Volvo that's pulling in to park. By the time Clare looks up, there's no stopping. Her blue Subaru plows into the rear of the green Mini Cooper like a battering ram, and the two cars meld together and slide into the intersection. The airbag belches a foul gas, and amid the jostling and heaving she hears scraping metal, screeching tires, and shattering glass. She wonders, *Am I going to die?* Then everything goes quiet.

She looks around for signs that she is dead, but sees none. She shakes her head clear and pushes her way out of the car. Inside the Mini Cooper, a heavily tattooed man wearing a *Duck Dynasty* beard and flannel shirt is sitting in the driver's seat, his arms draped around the passenger, a woman crying and holding her stomach. He looks at Clare and yells, "Call nine one one," then turns away. When Deputy Christie Truitt arrives on the scene three minutes later, Clare is still staring in the window of the Mini Cooper, watching the woman cry.

When the deputy approaches, the bearded man rolls down his window, and pleads, "My wife is pregnant, and the seatbelt tore up her stomach!"

The deputy turns and nods to Clare. "Are you okay?"

"I'm not injured if that's what you mean."

"Then go stand by your car. The paramedics will be with you as soon as they get here."

So Clare stands by her car—alone—and watches the woman in the Mini Cooper become the center of attention.

"Save my baby!" Aoife Murphy cries to the paramedics who swarm her.

"How far along is she?" one of them asks.

Her husband does some quick math. "Twenty-seven weeks."

Hearing "third trimester," the paramedics scramble to lift Aoife onto a stretcher, start an IV, and they load her into the ambulance. In a flash she is off to Lovejoy Medical Center, her belly hard as a rock with contractions, Aiden by her side. With the siren screeching, Aiden summons up the courage to ask, "Is our baby going to be all right?"

"We're doing all we can," is the only answer he gets.

With Aoife on her way, two paramedics convene around Clare, who has been waiting by herself. "That was quite a show," says Clare as one of them straps a blood pressure cuff on her arm.

The paramedic stops what he is doing. "What do you mean by that?"

"I mean you don't have to worry about me carrying on like that."

"She has a good reason to be upset. This is serious for a woman in her third trimester. Do you have children?"

"I have one, but he's adopted. Bringing a child into this world when there are so many children who already need a home is morally senseless." Clare zeroes in on his wedding band. "I'll bet you and the missus have kids, right?"

The paramedic glares at her. "I have three. Now let's get you checked out."

"Your vitals check out okay, but I recommend you go to the hospital just to be on the safe side. After all, this was more than a fender bender, and sometimes there are internal injuries we can't see."

"I'm not an invalid. I'll go as long as I don't have to lie down."

"You can sit up if you want."

As the paramedic starts to help her up into the ambulance, Clare remembers something. "I'll be right back," she says. She hoofs it over to the mangled Subaru, and there it is—her phone—lying on the floor next to the brake pedal. She opens it and the four letters *c-h-o-c* are staring her in the face. She looks over both shoulders.

Then pushes *Delete*.

On her way back to the ambulance, Deputy Truitt pulls

her aside. "What happened?"

"It was an accident."

"Whether it was an accident or not remains to be seen. Why didn't you stop?"

"I didn't have time. The dude slammed on his brakes. There was no way I could stop."

"Can you give a little more detail?"

"Like what?"

"Like how fast were you going? How close were you following? How come you didn't put on your brakes?"

"I told you: it was an accident. He slammed on his brakes, and there was no way I could stop. Is there anything else you want to know? Weather forecast? Stock market report? Nearest donut shop?"

"That's all for now," warns Truitt.

Minutes later, Clare is sitting in the back of the ambulance. They're not running with sirens on, so inside it's silent, though the paramedic opposite her keeps his eyes fixed on hers. "Is someone meeting you at the hospital?" he says at last.

"Like who?"

"I don't know. You're going to need a ride home. Is there someone in your family you can call?"

Clare purses her lips as though the paramedic just told a bad joke. "I'm an orphan. I don't have any family."

"No husband or boyfriend?"

Clare hesitates. "Not the last time I checked."

"So you're a single mother. Well, it's not good to be alone at times like this. You really should call someone."

"I wouldn't know who to call," says Clare. But when the paramedic turns his back to speak with the driver, she discretely taps a message to her partner, Libby.

Car accident, going to Lovejoy Medical. Get there ASAP!

The Arm of the Law

Libby frantically flies through the doors of the emergency room. "I'm looking for Clare McDowell. She was in a car accident. Can you help me find her? Please?" she says to the patient coordinator.

"What is your relationship with the patient?" asks the coordinator.

"I'm her closest friend. Libby Lockhart."

"Sorry. Only family members are allowed in the exam rooms. That's the policy. You're welcome to have a seat and wait for her."

"Wait a minute," says Libby. "I said we are friends, but she's really my cousin. Cousins first; friends second. Ask her, she'll vouch for me."

"I'll ask Dr. Murphy," says the coordinator, who disappears down the hall. She re-emerges a minute later. "You got lucky this time; Dr. Murphy doesn't know all the rules yet. Follow me." She leads Libby to an examination room where Clare is finishing up with the doctor. "Clare, your cousin is here," the coordinator announces.

"Cousin Libby!" muses Clare.

Dr. Murphy welcomes Libby into the exam room, smiling at the ruse. "Your cousin is going to be fine, but she needs to go home and rest."

Libby throws her arms around Clare and kisses her on the cheek. Clare stiffens.

"You're the woman that ran into my brother and sister-in-law, right?" the doctor says. "They took her upstairs to try and save the baby. I don't know what your spiritual beliefs are, but if you believe anything at all, pray. Cross your fingers. Knock on wood. It's touch and go for that baby. Now go home and get some rest."

The two women step into the hallway, and Libby takes Clare by the hand and leads her toward the exit. "What happened?" she whispers.

Clare whispers back. "This guy straight out of *Duck Dynasty* slams on his brakes, and the Subaru is totaled. I'll tell you the whole story when we get outside."

On the way out, they walk around a corner and find themselves face to face with Aiden Murphy, who is surrounded by a small army of distraught-looking family and friends. Libby can tell who these people are—the crowd is brimming with tattoos and beards—and she smells bad blood the moment their eyes meet hers. She clamps down on Clare's hand and pulls in the opposite direction. The two women don't get far, though—maybe three steps before the voice of Aiden Murphy booms out of the crowd.

"Our baby is dead," the beleaguered man pronounces.

Clare stops and pivots. "Are you talking to me?"

"Who do you think I'm talking to?"

"That's too bad about your baby, but I hope you don't think this was my fault."

Clare and Libby are surrounded: Dr. Brendan Murphy on one side and Aiden Murphy with his angry mob on the other. Libby is about to pee in her pants when out of nowhere, Deputy Truitt steps in and plants herself in the middle of the mob. "Everyone take a step back and cool down," she commands. She slowly backs Clare and Libby away from the mourners and tells Clare, "Wait for me in the lobby."

As they walk away, Libby turns to Aiden. "I'm sorry about your baby."

Clare crunches Libby's hand like a vice. "What are you doing?"

"I feel sorry for him."

"Just do what the deputy says and be quiet."

Libby pulls her hand out of Clare's grasp. "Back off, Clare. I'm here because I care."

A half hour later, Truitt finds Clare and Libby sitting on a sofa in the hospital lobby, Clare on one end, Libby on the other. The deputy sits down and turns to Clare. "Three witnesses say you had time to stop if you had put on the brakes. I have to ask again, why didn't you stop? Were you daydreaming? Are you taking medication? Maybe you were distracted by a phone call or text message?"

Clare looks as bewildered as the deputy. "I don't know. He slammed on his brakes and I couldn't stop. You can't blame me for that."

"If that's all you have to say, then my preliminary investigation is complete. My report will indicate that you are at fault for the accident. That's the law." Deputy Truitt hands Clare a traffic citation.

"I'm getting a ticket?" Clare refuses to reach out and take it.

"It's not a simple ticket. I am citing you for reckless driving. It's a misdemeanor, but you could get a two thousand-dollar fine and a year in jail. If the Prosecutor upgrades the charge to a felony, you could be looking at ten thousand dollars and ten years in prison. I've impounded your vehicle as evidence. I could arrest you right now, but I am going to release you on your own recognizance. If you fail to appear in court next Monday, a warrant will be issued for your arrest and I promise to come looking for you. Any questions?"

Clare grabs the ticket out of Deputy Truitt's hand. "I'll be there on Monday."

Wouldn't This Be a Good Time?

Clare emails the CEO at work that she has to take the day off for personal reasons and gives no explanation as to why.

On the way home, Clare asks Libby to swing by the pre-school to pick up Morton. Libby goes in and comes out with Morton holding her hand. The little boy scrambles into the car the way two-year-olds do. "Hi Mommy!"

Clare pulls Morton into her arms and holds him close. She brushes his face. "My precious boy. Thank God, you're safe." She straps him in, and double-checks the buckle on the car seat. And home they go.

That evening, Clare sits by herself in the back yard.

Nobody knows I was texting so why should I say I was? It wouldn't bring the baby back and would only make people angrier than they already are. People don't have a right to pry into my personal business.

Once Morton is in bed, Libby joins her in the back yard, thinking Clare may want to talk. They sit side by side on the picnic table.

"You've been through a lot today," says Libby.

"Yep."

"You must be upset."

"I have to decide what to tell people at the office," says Clare.

"Why not just tell them you were in a car accident and leave it at that?"

"Absolutely not. It's nobody's business!"

"Clare, please tell me you weren't texting when this happened. Because you know we've talked about that."

"I had no idea the dude was going to slam on his brakes! Alexa texted me about a stupid donut. I wasn't about to admit that to the cop. That deputy is bad news!"

Libby sighs, and they sit quietly for a while.

"I feel terrible for that poor couple," Libby says at last.

"Thanks a lot. As if I don't feel guilty enough already."

Libby bites her lip.

"So here's the deal: I don't want anyone to know about the accident, the ticket, the emergency room, nothing. I'll tell my boss that I came down with the flu on the way to work and had to turn around and go back home. Nobody can argue with the flu. The Subaru is totaled, so we'll get a new car tomorrow, and nobody needs to know what happened."

"My dad already knows about the accident. I called him the minute I found out."

"I should have known. Has he told anyone at Macklin Media?"

"You know he doesn't discuss anything personal at work—he hasn't even told anyone you and I are in a relationship."

"Well, don't tell anyone. And tell your dad not to tell anyone either—especially at work. This is my personal business and nobody else needs to know."

Libby softens her voice. "Since we're on the topic of parents, wouldn't this be a good time to get in touch with your dad? I think your parents would want to know. I mean, you've shunned them for seven years. How would you feel if Morton quit talking to you for seven years? Haven't you shut them out long enough?"

"Don't even go there. They don't care about me. I'm an orphan. I have to look out for myself."

"For God's sake, you're an orphan of your own choosing. You don't know how your parents feel about you. Why don't you give them a chance?"

"Look, I don't want anyone to know about this. If you care about me, you'll respect my privacy and stop bringing this up."

Not Guilty, Your Honor

It's Monday morning. Clare is on her way to Court in her brand-new Subaru. On the way, she tests out different spins on "Not guilty." She tries out, "Your Honor, as God is my witness, I am not guilty." *No sense bringing God into it.* "Reckless driving, Your Honor? I stand accused, but as an innocent woman!" *Too much like Scarlett O'Hara.* "Take these charges and shove 'em, Your Honor, because, I'm not guilty— hell no, not in a million years." *Never tell a judge to shove it.*

The minute Clare walks into the Courthouse, Danny Coscarelli shuffles her into a consultation room without even taking time to introduce himself. He comes highly recommended by her insurance company, but this is her first time meeting him, and Clare figures she deserves some basic manners.

"I've got good news and bad news," he tells her. "The bad news is that the prosecutor has added the charge of vehicular feticide. It's a new law—the killing of a viable fetus with a car—and she's dying to make an example of you. You could get ten years in prison."

Clare wants to scream, *Ten years over a donut?* but instead says, "Hello Mr. Coscarelli. My name is Clare McDowell. What a pleasure to meet you. (Nice to meet you, too, Clare.) Thank you for the bad news. (You are welcome.) Do you have any good news for me, Mr. Coscarelli?"

"Sorry to be rude. The good news is that the prosecutor is offering a deal. If you will plead guilty to reckless driving today and get it over with, she will drop the vehicular feticide charge and ask the Judge for a five thousand-dollar fine and a thirty day jail term that you can serve on weekends. That's pretty generous on her part, and you should consider taking the deal. Reckless driving is only a misdemeanor. You can keep your job, keep your driver's license, and pay off your fine in monthly installments. All you'd be giving up is your weekends for four months."

"Sorry, but I wasn't driving recklessly, and pleading guilty would be a miscarriage of justice. Aiden Murphy caused this accident, not me."

Mr. Coscarelli looks Clare in the eye. "I'm afraid the prosecutor will be out for blood; this vehicular feticide law is for the benefit of pregnant women and their unborn children. Everyone will be on the side of women and babies. If you're found guilty, the prosecutor will push for prison time out of respect for Aoife Murphy and her deceased baby."

"I didn't do anything wrong, and I'm not going to say I did. I'm an orphan, and I have to look out for myself."

Coscarelli sighs. "Clare, we can go in there and plead not guilty if that's what you want. But if this thing goes to trial, I have to explain to the jury exactly what happened and show that it couldn't have been avoided. Why didn't you put on the brakes?"

"I didn't put on the brakes because I didn't have time."

Mr. Coscarelli takes a deep breath and glances at the ceiling. "If you want me to defend you, you have to come up with something better than that."

"All I can tell you is that Aiden Murphy slammed on his brakes and I didn't have time to stop."

"You're a broken record, Clare. I know you don't think you did anything wrong. But we are talking about ten years in prison here. That's a long time to stare at four walls. I know this prosecutor, and she will come after you with a vengeance if you tempt her. It's your call. We can go in and plead not guilty, but I'm warning you: you'll need to come up with a better explanation than what I've heard so far."

Fifteen minutes later, Clare rises to her feet and listens to the prosecutor call out the charges: reckless driving and vehicular feticide. She hangs on to the edge of the table and, without elaboration, answers, "Not guilty, Your Honor."

"You've requested trial by a jury of your peers, Ms. McDowell. Those proceedings will commence in this courtroom, at nine o'clock ten weeks from today. Court is adjourned." The gavel sounds and the clock starts counting down.

Matti Makkonen

A month goes by. Clare hasn't told a single soul about the accident—her friends, coworkers, and neighbors are in the dark. Except for Libby, nobody knows she was texting—not even Mr. Coscarelli—and Clare is resolved to take her secret to the grave.

The secret won't leave her alone, though. At work, she googles *Who invented texting*, and wastes an entire day wondering whether the now-deceased Matti Makkonen passed away in remorse over the death and destruction he indirectly caused on the roadways of the world. At home, she falls into a panic because Morton didn't say "I love you" when she put him to bed. *He's two years old; isn't he old enough to know that he might not get another chance to tell his mother he loves her?* In her car, Clare is trapped in a world of phone-talkers, speeders, traffic-weavers, and texters—all of whom are seconds away from killing someone.

On Saturday morning, Clare is in the front yard raking grass when Libby's father, Burt Lockhart, stops by for a visit. Burt is head of security at Macklin Media—that's how Clare met Libby in the first place. Burt is six-foot-four, and he has learned to be especially gentle with his movements and language, so as not to intimidate those smaller than him, which is just about everyone. He drives a big SUV and after he parks in front of the house, he picks up his phone and checks his messages. Then he puts the phone down and opens the car door. Clare can hardly believe her eyes. As Burt exits his SUV, she slams the rake on the ground and stomps into the house where she finds Libby and Morton watching *Scooby-Doo*.

"Unbelievable! Your dad just pulled up in front of the house, texting the whole time, not paying attention to his driving," she clamors.

Before Libby can say a word, in walks Burt, and Clare screams at him. "You're dangerous! There could have been kids playing in the street, and you wouldn't have seen them. You're going to kill someone. You're going to kill a child, like Morton. You're going to kill a whole family."

Burt just stands there. They all stare at one another until Clare runs upstairs and locks the bedroom door behind her. Morton starts crying and runs to Libby who scoops him into her arms and tells him it's okay.

"What's going on?" asks Burt.

"Too hard to explain," Libby responds, "and we're not supposed to talk about it, I guess. It's getting a little weird around here."

"This too shall pass," says Burt, and the conversation turns lighter.

"How are the Braves doing?" asks Libby.

"They're trying to get out of the basement. But they better get some better pitchers." Baseball is always good for a change of topic.

After Burt leaves, Clare comes back out of the bedroom and enters the kitchen. Libby is fixing lunch for Morton. Clare confronts her: "So you're saying it's okay to play with your phone when you're driving?"

"What are you talking about?"

"I'm talking about you giving your dad a free pass to run over innocent children. You're saying that if he runs over Morton, it's okay."

"Come on, Clare. You're losing your mind. I'm not saying it's okay, but it didn't happen. He didn't run over Morton. He has never run over anyone. He has never even caused a car accident."

"It's only a matter of time. I don't want Morton riding in the car with him. I mean it. And I don't want Burt coming over when I'm here. Invite him when I'm not here. I'm under a lot of pressure right now, *in case you can't tell*."

"I'm not going to kick my father out of my life because you don't like the way he drives. Be careful who you're talking about. He's my father; I love him as much as I love you. He loves you like you're his own daughter. And he has been an amazing grandfather to Morton."

"The fact that he is your father has nothing to do with it!"

"It has everything to do with it. You're trying to do the same thing you did to your parents. You were a nervous wreck about coming out when you met me, and you projected your anxiety on to your parents. You felt hurt, and you blamed them. Okay, your parents aren't perfect. They didn't understand what it's like to be a lesbian. How could they? But they were trying to understand. They weren't judging us. They didn't intend to hurt you. Then *poof!* You just ghosted them out of your life. Problem solved. Seven years gone. They've never even met Morton. It's wrong, Clare, and I'm not going to do it to my dad."

Clare runs back upstairs and locks the door, and Libby takes Morton to the park. Later that afternoon, with Morton down for a nap, Libby sits by herself in the back yard and weeps.

The Return of Truitt

The clock is moving fast now; only five days until the trial begins. Clare walks into work at Macklin Media only to have Alexa Arioli drag her into the conference room. She locks the door. "I had a visitor this morning. Her name is Christie Truitt, and she's—"

"I know who she is, but why would she be contacting you?"

"She found me through your phone records. She wanted to know about a text message I sent a couple of months ago."

"Donut Day," says Clare.

"Donut Day? You mean accident day, don't you? She says you were in a car accident. You never told me that; you said you had the flu. Do you realize that my sister Maria is related to Aiden and Aoife Murphy? I had no idea you were the one that hit them. This deputy claims you were texting when you had the accident."

"What did you tell her?"

"What could I tell her? She had the phone records right in front of her."

"Right, but the fact that we texted doesn't prove I was texting when the accident happened. The message you sent was way before the accident. Believe me, texting didn't cause the accident."

"Well, I got slapped with a subpoena, and I have to go to Court next Monday. I'll have to get a new dress and everything."

"Poor girl, I feel so sorry for you. You didn't tell Ms. Macklin about this, did you? I could get in trouble."

"I haven't told anybody, but I don't appreciate being implicated in the death of a baby. Aiden and Aoife were pretty torn up. My sister told me how hard it's been for them. This is pretty low, even by my standards."

"Like it or not, you are implicated. I didn't ask you to text me, and I didn't care about the stupid donut anyway. Don't feel guilty, though. That accident had nothing to do with texting. I swear the text happened *before* the accident. Just remember that when you get on the stand next Monday."

"I'm not supposed to be talking to you about this, so don't say another word." Alexa turns and marches out of the room.

People Want You to Lie

Two days until the trial. Clare can't sleep—can't eat anything but cookies. And she feels like everyone is pointing the finger at her—even Libby.

It's Saturday, and Libby is driving Morton over to Grandpa's (since Clare won't allow Burt to pick him up.) When Clare is certain that Libby has dropped Morton off, and is on her way back home, she sends Libby a text.

planting flowers in back yard

Then she hides behind the fence where she can spy on Libby when she pulls in the drive. Libby pulls in and heads straight to the back yard. Clare locks and loads. Libby walks into the back yard, and Clare opens fire: "You knew I was in the back yard. You read my text while you were driving!"

Clare runs for the bedroom, but this time Libby chases her. "I'm not stupid. You're putting up a wall to me like you do everyone else. But it's not going to work. You can't dump your problems on people and then boot them out of your life. If you keep driving people away, you are going to end up all alone."

"I am alone!" shouts Clare.

"Stop saying that. And don't start that orphan bullshit. You have people who care about you if you would just let them. You are not going to push me away like you did your parents. I won't let you. So stop it, for God's sake. Come over here, now, and tell me why you can't let people love you."

"I can't do it!"

"Clare, if you don't do it now, you will never do it. Just try to trust me. What do you think I'm going to do? Kill you? Die on you? What's the barrier? We're not talking life and death here. We're just talking about basic trust. Trust is not going to kill you."

"I'll try. But don't ask me to get all touchy-feely. I can't do that. I'm a cactus. I hurt people. And I know it. If you want to call it a wall, okay, I've had a wall around me since I was twelve. Nobody wanted to hear that I liked girls. So I lied. I lied to boys. I lied to girls. I lied to my parents. I lied to everyone. And I believed my own lies. Now, my life is one huge, monumental lie. Have you noticed that people are happier when you lie? Look what happened at the hospital—that patient coordinator forced you to lie and was happy when you did! So I build walls to protect myself . . .there are worse things in the world, Libby. Get over it."

"Look, the world has changed. Lesbians don't have to lie anymore. You and I are a family. Nobody can take that away from us. Let people in; at least, let me in."

Libby tries to brush Clare's hair, but Clare stiffens up as though she has *rigor mortis*.

The Pursuit of Justice

Clare and Libby pull up outside the courthouse. Danny Coscarelli is waiting for them in the parking lot, which is practically full. Libby hops out and looks around. "Something big must be going on here today."

Mr. Coscarelli pays Libby no attention, so Clare says, "This is my partner, Libby Lockhart."

"Nice to meet you," is all the lawyer says.

"I better go find my dad; he's waiting inside," says Libby. She kisses Clare on the cheek and Clare stiffens. "Whatever happens today, keep your head up! I'll be sitting right behind you; I'm in your corner, Clare. I'm there for you. Good luck."

Mr. Coscarelli leads Clare into a conference room. "I'm calling this the 'nobody knows' defense. The prosecutor has to prove beyond a shadow of a doubt that your texting caused the accident. That's a hard thing to prove, and I don't think she can. Maybe she can prove you sent a text on your way to work, but she can't prove you were texting at the exact moment of the crash. My plan is to poke holes in their case and keep reminding the jury that nobody knows what caused the accident. I don't know—you don't know—they don't know. In the end, if even one juror says, 'Nobody knows,' you're off the hook."

Clare walks into the Courtroom and feels her knees buckle. The courtroom is packed with tattoos, beards, news reporters, and over a hundred young mothers and mothers-to-be. She grabs Danny's arm and holds on for dear life. "Why are all these people here?" she whispers.

"Behold the power of Facebook," Danny whispers back. "They formed a group to make you an example of what happens to drivers who crash into pregnant women."

"I had no idea. They really hate me, don't they?"

"They don't even know you, Clare. It's social media; they

hate what they're told to hate. Don't worry, I'm going to put a big dent in their plans. Don't pay attention to them."

Of course, Clare can't help but pay attention. Every eye in the crowd is staring at her, every nose bent out of shape, every tooth ready to rip her apart. Nobody is on her side—except for one person. Burt is scrunched in the fourth row, saving a seat for Libby, surrounded by young mothers. He grins and flashes a thumbs up to Clare.

He loves you like his own daughter.

"Where is Libby?" mouths Clare, but Burt shrugs his shoulders.

The bailiff bellows out, "In the matter of the People versus Clare McDowell. All rise!" The judge makes his entrance, wearing a stately black robe. Next, the twelve jurors march in—ten women and two men who will decide whether the "nobody knows" defense will fly or not. Clare takes comfort when she sees that neither of the male jurors have beards, although two of the women jurors look like camouflage is their favorite color.

"American justice is amazing. I did a good job with the jury selection," says Danny, sporting a very smug smile.

The prosecutor calls the first witness: "Will Aiden Murphy please take the stand?" Clare has never seen a flannel shirt under a suit before, but she has to admit that the rattlesnake boots are a sharp touch.

On the stand, Aiden recounts what happened on that fateful day. "I looked in my rear-view mirror, and I saw a blue Subaru following me at a distance. I had no choice but to slow down for a Volvo that was parking. And the next thing I know, my car blasted off like a rocket into the intersection. My first thought was 'What could possibly have hit me?' since the blue Subaru surely would have seen me stop. It was like she didn't know where her brake pedal was. She didn't even try to stop!" Aiden slams his fist down on his knee.

"Don't worry, I can take care of him," Coscarelli whispers to Clare.

He stands up. "The fact is, Mr. Murphy, that you don't know why the defendant didn't stop, do you?"

"I can guess."

"You can guess—anyone can guess—but you weren't in her car, so you don't really know, do you? Answer yes or no."

"I don't know," the angry man concedes.

"No further questions, Your Honor."

Next, the prosecutor calls Aoife Murphy to the stand. Aoife is wearing a blue and white retro print dress. Like something out of June Cleaver's 1950's, it has an oversized collar that seems to project the sanctity of motherhood. Aoife tells a moving story. "We put every ultrasound photo of our baby on the refrigerator. We were watching him grow and develop. Then one day Aiden and I sat down to pick his name. We wanted to follow our Irish heritage, so we named him Ciaran, spelled the Irish way. As he got bigger and bigger, we decorated his room and filled it with toys." Her eyes fill with tears. "To this day, those toys are still in his room—a room he will never know. But I don't have the heart to take them out."

The judge says, "Mrs. Murphy, please take a moment before you continue." He motions the bailiff to bring her a box of tissues. Tissues are coming out all over the courtroom, including among the Jurors.

Aoife composes herself. "Now I have learned the cruelest reality. Ciaran doesn't have a birth certificate because he wasn't officially born. He doesn't have a death certificate, either, because he didn't legally die. My little Ciaran is a medical and legal non-event—eternally stuck in limbo as if he never existed. It's harsh because he is and always will be my baby. Nobody can take him away from me." There are sobs throughout the courtroom, and Mr. Coscarelli is relieved to see tears in Clare's eyes too.

Aoife again regains her composure, and the prosecutor asks her, "Mrs. Murphy, can you point to the person who rear-ended you on that horrific day?"

Aoife's forearm rises slowly, as though this is the most difficult thing she has ever had to do. Her arm lunges forward like a gun barrel aimed at Clare. "That's the woman who killed my baby!"

The courtroom erupts and the Judge shouts, "Order in the court!"

Mr. Coscarelli flies to his feet. "Your Honor, the defense is sympathetic to the loss Mrs. Murphy has suffered, but that last statement is inflammatory. I ask that it be stricken from the record."

"Mrs. Murphy, you are not allowed to say things like that. Just answer the questions yes or no. The jury will disregard that statement," the judge exhorts.

"That's the one statement every person on the jury is going to remember," Coscarelli whispers to Clare. "I have to be gentle with her."

He turns back to Aoife. "Mrs. Murphy, my client, the defendant, is truly sorry that your baby miscarried, and I'm sure everyone in the courtroom wishes this had not happened. But the truth is, you don't really know why your baby miscarried, do you? Many factors could have played a part. I understand you have high blood pressure. Maybe you have an undiagnosed illness. Maybe you were stressed out that day even before the accident. From a medical viewpoint, the causes of miscarriage and stillbirth are often unknown and hard to detect."

"I know who killed my baby," Aoife snarls.

"Move to strike!" Mr. Coscarelli exclaims, and the judge again admonishes Aoife.

"No further questions," says Mr. Coscarelli. But one look at the jury confirms what Mr. Coscarelli has already said; they are not going to forget Aoife Murphy. Clare will never forget her either.

Clare turns and looks for Libby, but the seat next to Burt is still empty. Libby promised, "You are not alone!" But Clare feels she is.

Next up for the prosecution is Deputy Christie Truitt. Deputy Truitt left her brown uniform hanging in the closet today and instead chose a crisp, navy-blue suit. She's animated, and Clare can't help but think she seems like an astrophysicist as she describes the angles of the Subaru vis-à-vis the Mini Cooper as they collided and rocketed their way into the intersection. She goes into great detail explaining the meanings of boost power, weight equations, and angle trajectories. She cites damage reports showing scratch marks and the bend of metal, and shows photos that indicate not a single skid mark was made on the pavement prior to the impact.

But the prosecutor mistakenly summarizes this with the wrong question. "Deputy Truitt, in your expert opinion, was the defendant's reckless driving the approximate cause of death of Ciaran Murphy?"

"That's a medical question I'm not qualified to answer," Truitt responds.

"She just made a big mistake," Coscarelli whispers.

The prosecutor hands Truitt the event data recorder, the so-called black box from Clare's Subaru. "Deputy, using the data from this black box, were you able to determine the exact time that the defendant's vehicle collided with the Murphy's?"

"Yes. The collision occurred at exactly six minutes past eight," replies the Deputy.

"No further questions," says the prosecutor.

Danny Coscarelli stands a little too quickly. "Deputy Truitt," he blurts, "you seem capable. If I am ever a victim in a traffic accident, I'd like to have you lead the investigation. You know your stuff."

"Thank you," replies the deputy.

"In fact, you know a lot about what happened on the morning of the accident—maybe more than Mr. and Mrs. Murphy, maybe more than my client, Ms. McDowell. But the one thing you don't know is why the defendant didn't apply the brakes. Isn't that correct?"

"I have my ideas," replies the deputy.

"You have ideas. I have ideas. Everyone in the courtroom has ideas. In America, everyone has the right to an opinion, don't they? But after hearing all your scientific analysis, the fact is that not a single person in this courtroom knows with absolute certainty why the defendant didn't stop. Do you know with absolute certainty why she didn't stop?"

"With absolute certainty, no. I don't. Not for sure."

"No further questions, Your Honor."

Clare turns to Danny. "Don't you need to poke a few holes in her testimony?"

"How?" asks the lawyer. "She's an excellent witness, and her testimony is killing you. The best thing to do is get her off the stand before she hurts you more. Trust me. I still think we're going to win."

Again, Clare looks for Libby. Burt is there, but Libby is nowhere to be seen.

"The Prosecution calls Alexa Arioli to the stand." Alexa steps into the Courtroom, and parades to the witness stand like there is a spotlight following her. Alexa appears to be a reluctant witness at best; even her attire suggests she would rather be elsewhere. She's wearing a red dress that you would expect to see at a party, not in a courtroom.

"Do you swear to tell the whole truth and nothing but the truth?" asks the bailiff.

"I'll give it my best shot," says Alexa.

"Let's try that again," says the judge. So the bailiff asks the question a second time.

"Ms. Arioli, take the gum out of your mouth, answer 'I do,' and mean it."

"I do."

The Prosecutor hands Alexa a stack of papers. "Ms. Arioli, these are the defendant's phone records. I'd like you to turn to the second page, and tell the jury if that is your phone number there."

"Looks like it to me," says Alexa.

"Answer yes or no," the judge tells her.

"Okay," she says.

"Yes or no? Is that your phone number on page two?"

"That looks like my number."

The judge intervenes again. "Ms. Arioli, if it looks like your number, then it is your number. Correct?"

"Yes, Your Honor. It looks like my number."

The judge pats his forehead and breathes heavily. "Let the record show that the phone number on page two is, in fact, Ms. Arioli's number—now let's move on."

"Can you tell the jury whether you remember sending a text message to the defendant on the morning of the accident, and if so, what did the message say?"

"You might say I asked her what kind of donut she wanted."

Now the prosecutor rubs her forehead. "Ms. Arioli, it doesn't matter what I would say. The question is what would you say?"

"Give a straight answer," the judge orders.

"I would say that I asked her what kind of donut she wanted." Alexa grins.

"What kind of donut," the prosecutor parrots. "And did you receive a response from the defendant?"

"She wanted chocolate; Clare always wants chocolate. I figured she wanted chocolate, but I had to ask for sure."

"A chocolate donut." The prosecutor rolls her eyes.

"Okay, Ms. Arioli. Will you look at the phone record and tell the jury what time you and the defendant exchanged these texts?"

Alexa looks at the document. "Six minutes past eight."

The courtroom buzzes with whispers, and Alexa seems to be the only one in the room who doesn't know why.

The judge bangs his gavel. "This is my last warning. Spectators who can't be quiet will be ushered out of the courtroom. Do I make myself clear?"

"No further questions, Your Honor."

Danny Coscarelli prances up to Alexa like she is an old family friend—his manner is shockingly cozy considering this is a witness who may hold the key to him winning or losing this case.

"Ms. Arioli, a minute is a long time, don't you think?"

"That depends on what you're doing in that minute," Alexa flips back to him.

"You're right. A lot can happen in a minute, can't it?"

"Some of the sweetest things in my life have happened in a minute or less."

"So it would be impossible to know whether the text messages you exchanged with the defendant actually caused the accident. They could have happened forty or fifty seconds before the accident. Would you agree?"

"I would agree. Some things in life we will never know."

"For all you know, those text messages had nothing to do with the accident. Isn't that true?"

"Honestly, I didn't even know Clare was in an accident until a few days ago. In my opinion, my text to her did not cause the accident."

"Thank you, Ms. Arioli. No further questions, Your Honor."

Coscarelli goes back to his table, and the judge stares him down. He had, after all, been just a little too smooth. Just the same, Danny smiles at Clare. "We just won. There's a Grand Canyon full of doubt here. The prosecutor hasn't proved a thing."

Clare breathes a sigh of relief, for the first time in nearly three months.

"Your Honor, the prosecution calls Libby Lockhart to the stand."

Coscarelli jumps out of his chair. "Your Honor, I object to the prosecution calling this witness. Libby Lockhart has no first-hand knowledge of the accident; she wasn't even there."

"Your Honor, we believe that Ms. Lockhart will be able to shed light on the accident in a way that no first-hand observer could. We believe she has knowledge about the accident straight out the defendant's mouth."

"Your Honor, Libby Lockhart is the defendant's intimate partner; they have been in a relationship for seven years. It's like a marriage. Private communication between married couples is privileged, and that same privilege should apply to this couple. Ms. Lockhart should not be compelled to testify."

"Your Honor, the Prosecution concedes that if the defendant and Ms. Lockhart were married, then the witness should not be required to testify. We point to one simple fact, though. They are not legally married, and the right not to testify is reserved for married couples only."

"Your Honor, same-sex couples were only recently granted the right to marry. It would be wrong to penalize them for this. It's a violation of my client's constitutional right to love whoever she chooses. I ask the court to rule that Libby Lockhart cannot be forced to testify."

The judge reflects for a minute, and then rules: "I agree that it's a violation of the defendant's constitutional right to love whoever she chooses. But that is a matter for another court on another day. In the matter before this Court, the law prevails. The objection is overruled; Libby Lockhart is called to the witness stand."

Moments later, Deputy Christie Truitt ushers Libby into the courtroom and leads her to the witness stand as though to the gallows. Several spectators in the crowded courtroom point and stare. One look at Libby and you know she wasn't expecting to be on the witness stand today: she is wearing a green sweatshirt, jeans, and sneakers.

On the stand, Libby takes in the faces of the twelve jurors who will decide not only Clare's fate, but hers as well. She raises her right hand.

"Do you swear to tell the whole truth and nothing but the truth?"

Libby sighs. "I do."

The prosecutor begins. "Ms. Lockhart, you are in a personal relationship with the defendant, isn't that right?"

"Yes. We are a family. We have been together for seven years; we have a son named Morton."

"A family, as you put it, so I assume that you and the defendant engage in private conversations. Is that correct?"

"Of course we do," Libby snaps.

"So, has the defendant has ever told you that she was texting when she collided with the car occupied by Aiden and Aoife Murphy?"

"I wasn't there; I don't know anything about the accident."

The judge intervenes. "Ms. Lockhart, you must answer the question whether you want to or not. Otherwise, I will have to send you to jail for contempt. I don't want to do that, but I will. Please answer the question yes or no."

"Ms. Lockhart, did the defendant at any time tell you that she was texting at the time of the accident?"

The courtroom is so quiet that Clare can hear her own heartbeat. Libby shifts in her seat, glances at the Judge, and surveys the Jury. Then she looks at Clare. *Lesbians don't have to lie anymore. We're a family now. Nobody can take that away from us.*

Libby looks the Prosecutor in the whites of her eyes, and confidently pronounces: "Yes, she did tell me that. We *are* a family."

The prosecutor stammers, and shakes her head. "Did I hear you correctly? Are you saying that the defendant told you she was texting when she ran into the Murphy's vehicle? Is that your testimony?"

"You heard me. Yes, she did. And I said *we are a family*." Libby turns to the court reporter and boldly says, "Make sure you get that last sentence."

Danny Coscarelli turns to Clare, whose eyes are glazed over, and whispers, "We have a problem. The 'Nobody knows' defense only works when nobody really knows."

Then he says, "Your Honor, I have no questions for Ms. Lockhart."

A Lot to Catch Up On

It's Visitation Day at the Southern Region Women's Correctional Facility, and Libby is freaking out: it's just as hard to get into this place as it would be to escape. And the guards rule. First, they frisk her entire body to make sure she isn't carrying contraband. Then she walks through a scanner, showing the guards every orifice of her body. Next, they weigh her so they can recheck her weight when she leaves to make sure she isn't carrying anything out. She goes through all this, just to sit with Clare for one hour in a room with unadorned concrete walls and steel tables bolted to the floor. No physical contact is allowed—a rule that is going to be difficult for a toucher like Libby.

"Thanks for coming. I thought maybe you wouldn't show after what I put you through," says Clare.

"Hey, it's only a seven-hour drive each way. I can get here and back in a day if I leave the house by four-thirty in the morning. Besides, we're a family. We've had to fight for it, and as far as I'm concerned we're sticking together, no matter what. Three years isn't that long, if you think about it."

Clare smiles. Libby always looks on the bright side of everything.

"How is Morton?"

"Morton is Morton. He's doing as well as can be expected. He cries for you sometimes. I tell him you're on a trip and that you'll be home before he knows it. Whatever you do, keep calling him. I put a poster of you up in his room so he can see your face every day."

"How's he doing at preschool?"

"I had to take him out of the school; it was too expensive. My dad takes care of him while I'm at work. He's paying half the mortgage for us. I don't know what we would do without him."

"Tell Burt I appreciate the care packages he sends. I feel alone in this place. You find out who really loves you when you go to prison."

They are silent for a moment. Then Libby says, "The trial got pretty crazy. Truitt was waiting for me at the front door of the courthouse. I didn't have a choice, you know."

"I know. And I know you had to tell the truth. I'm learning how important truth is. I'm learning the hard way, but better late than never." She forces a smile.

"I thought about lying on the stand. But I couldn't. I remembered all the times I've said, 'We have to be who we are—we can't live a lie.' I knew if I lied, it would be the end of you and me. We're a couple because we live the truth. I couldn't go back to lying again."

"It's ironic. The one thing I didn't want anyone to know is the one thing everyone ended up knowing. Why you stay with me, I'll never know."

"I told you and I mean it. I am never going to kick you out of my life. I take the good with the bad. I know some people think I'm a fool, but loyalty counts for something in my book. We had to fight to be a couple, and I'm just not going to let anyone take that away from me—not even you."

"I don't want to be alone anymore. Once I get out of here . . . "

The guard abruptly interrupts and says, "Your hour is over."

Libby submits to the same searches she endured to get in, and once she gets back outside, she takes a deep breath and stretches her arms. Freedom has never felt so precious to her. She takes the long walk to her car, and halfway across the parking lot she can hardly believe her eyes: a man and woman are rushing towards her, waving and calling her name. Libby hardly knows what to say. "What are you doing here?" she sputters.

"We're here to visit Clare," says the woman.

"Visit Clare? Are you sure she wants to see you?"

"She wrote us a letter and asked us to come. So we're here. Maybe Clare thinks we disapprove of her, but we don't—we never did."

"It was a difficult time for all of us. I wasn't always as kind toward you as I should have been," says Libby.

"Things were said that didn't need to be said, but there are no hard feelings. We love Clare; we lost her, and now she's alive again. Hey, we have to hurry inside."

"I hope you have a good visit," says Libby. She takes a few steps, then turns back. "Dr. and Mrs. McDowell, would you like to meet your grandson, Morton? Maybe you can come over next week and have dinner with us. A lot has happened in the last seven years. We have a lot to catch up on."

CORRESPONDENCE

Dear Dad and Trudy,

I can't tell you how much I appreciate you sending the books. I could hardly believe it, after all this time of not seeing you. I'm sorry they sent the hardcovers back; we're not allowed to have hardcovers. I guess they could be used as a weapon or something. Or maybe they want us to be stupid. Many of the women here can't read, so you'd think they would want us to read whether it's a hard or soft cover, but this isn't the Hilton—there's a rule for everything. If someone gets a letter on perfumed paper, they send that back, too, and you don't even get to read it. Don't forget. My number has to be after my name on the envelope and in the letter. For the next three years, I am Clare McDowell #516468. I better get used to it.

Guess who visited me? The priest! Father Miles Joyce came by and stayed for four hours (clergy can stay as long as they want.) I think he came with the idea of counseling me, but once I found out he's a *Game of Thrones* guy, it's all he and I could talk about. According to the warden, Father Miles created quite a stir. You guessed it: the Harley. They've never had a priest show up on a motorcycle before, so they were suspicious, and did a strip search. (If you ever choose to visit, I don't think they would do a strip search of you). Anyway, it seems that the Holy Father has a cross tattooed on his back. At least that's what the warden claims, but one of the guards told me Miles has a couple more tattoos in hidden places. Too much information, I would say. That priest is so dopey. Used to be, a priest speaking to me made my skin crawl, but I have to admit, even though I've only been here a few days, the loneliness is unbearable, and any face from Lovejoy is welcome.

I'm sounding negative again. Father Miles says I need to stop looking for the worst in everyone. He wants me to focus on seeing the best in people. So I guess I better get back to exactly *why* I am writing this letter.

Oh, remember, they read every letter, so don't write anything they can use against me. The guards like to get an edge on you when they have personal info to throw in your face, so please be careful. I don't want them nicknaming me *Lizzy* if you know what I mean. I'm not going to feel ashamed or lie about who I am—anymore—but I don't want it used against me. (They will probably delete this paragraph, but it is what it is and they do whatever they want.)

Okay, I'm writing because Father Miles says I should talk to you about this and listen to what you have to say. You know I'm not good with words, so it's probably just as well that I have to write it. That way I won't get too emotional. Trudy, what I'm about to say involves you too, so bear up and cut me some slack, please. I don't intend to be difficult; but being difficult seems to be what I do best, whether I want to or not. The priest says I need to work on getting along with people, and I am trying.

This has been eating at me since I was seven years old, so here it goes:

Dad, when I was growing up, you were always there for me. You came to all my events, sat through my band concerts, coached my softball team—you name it, you did it. So I can't fault you for that. But—and this is a pretty big but . . .

When Mom died, I lost my trust in you. You were a doctor and in my eyes, I thought you could have saved her. Through the years so many people I met would say, "Your father saved my life." But all I could think was how you didn't even save your own wife. You heal people all the time, but you let my mother die. Maybe it was just the naïveté of a seven-year-old, but my attitude was, *What kind of doctor can't save his own family?*

That morning you walked in my bedroom, sat on the bed, and told me, "Your mom isn't coming home this time." I didn't know what you meant. You weren't crying, so I had no way of knowing she was *never* coming home. You could have said, "Your mother died this morning." But you didn't. And for the rest of that day, I was waiting for you to explain where she was going. If she wasn't coming home, I thought she was going somewhere—somewhere to get better, maybe going somewhere I could visit her. Maybe I was a fool. Or maybe I was just seven. It was a long time ago.

I didn't figure out that Mom died until later that evening when Uncle Jim told me my mom was in heaven. It hit me like a ton of bricks. *Heaven? Heaven is where dead people go. That can't be, because my mom isn't dead. She's just not coming home yet.* "No," I told him, "My mom is in the hospital. She's going to get better." But the look on his face told me it was true.

I felt betrayed. Here was Uncle Jim telling me the truth, and I don't even like him. I couldn't cry in front of him. You could have cried when you sat on my bed. I know you're a doctor and that you deal with death all the time; I know your patients don't want to see you cry. But my mother died and you didn't cry. Did it not occur to you that I was only seven years old? For God's sake, my mom was dead and you didn't cry. So how was I supposed to feel? I started hating everyone that day. Especially you. God, too. What kind of God would take my mom away from me and send her to heaven? Was the big man playing Russian Roulette and me and my mom just happened to be the losers?

After the funeral—the worst day of my life (yes, worse than going to prison)—you promised that you and I would stick together. You said that we would always have each other. You told me you loved me, and I believed you and clung to you. You were all I had. I know you did your best to hold your practice together and still be home for me in the afternoons and evenings, but that image of you not crying—Dr. Straight face—stuck in my memory. You loved Mom too, and look what happened to her? For years, I lay in bed at night with one question eating away at me: if I were to die, would you cry? To this day, over twenty years later, I still wonder about that.

But to get back to why I am writing. When Trudy came into the picture, things got better for you but worse for me. You said I was your girl, and then along came Trudy. She made you happy. She made you laugh. She made you forget about Mom. I know that Trudy tried to get close to me, but her presence made me a third wheel. She stole you away from me. You didn't need me anymore—you had Trudy. Trudy had you. But who did I have? Nobody but myself.

In my heart, I was an orphan—left behind, frozen in time. To this day, despite the love that Libby and my little boy, Morton, have for me, I am quick to throw the first stone before anyone throws one at me.

If it's any consolation, I've had some time to think in here. Father Miles asked me if I might be the one with a heart of stone, not you. Maybe I'm the one who wouldn't cry if *you* died. I'm starting to think maybe he's right. I feel cold as a stone some days, and I throw a lot of stones, don't I? I feel ashamed of the way I treated that poor Irish couple. I would handle it differently now, but that's easy to say in hindsight, isn't it? I'm just starting to understand myself. And I'm doing my time. Paying my penance.

I think that Father Miles has touched on something though. I am a hypocrite. I want others to cut me slack when I need it, but I don't cut much slack for anyone around me. Father Miles says there are no free rides, that you and many others have paid a high price for my rides. I had never thought about that before.

Now I've had my say and bared my soul. Feel free to respond, and if you're worried about me getting into an argument with you, don't. I'm under strict orders from Father Miles to shut my mouth and listen, to not argue or get defensive. So write back if you can. Or feel free to visit me here in my new home. Of course, I'll understand if you don't.

You probably think I'm writing simply because I'm stuck in prison and want something. Well, you're not far off: I want another chance to be a family again. It's a lot to expect, I know. But it doesn't hurt to ask.

Your loving daughter,

Clare McDowell #516468

THE MUD RUN

It Sounds Dirty

Maria takes a deep breath, but before she can blow out the candles, her sister Alexa jumps in. "Hold it! I want to get a picture of the birthday girl."

Maria turns her head and waves her sister aside. "I don't want my picture taken."

So her mom butts in. "Come on, Maria. It won't kill you. I want to put it on Facebook. Our friends will never believe how grown up you girls are; it's like you were born yesterday."

Maria storms down the hallway. "Stay put," Liam tells everyone, and follows Maria to the bedroom, where he finds her pacing like a caged lion.

"What's going on?" he asks.

"I don't want my picture taken. My hair looks like shit. I look terrible."

"What are you talking about? You look amazing."

"I knew you wouldn't understand."

Suddenly, Tegan, squirrels across the bedroom floor, Aunt Alexa hot on his tail. "Okay, I'll settle for a picture of the three of you. Liam, put your arm around Maria.

Tegan, stand in front of your mom and dad. Smile!"

Bam, a photo of the perfect family is posted straight to Facebook.

"Get out of here," Maria chides her sister. "And take Tegan with you."

"Come on," Liam says. "It's your birthday. You're supposed to be having fun. Let's not wreck it."

"While we're at it, why did you invite Dr. and Mrs. McDowell when you knew that Aoife and Aiden were going to be here? You know Clare McDowell killed their baby. How do you think they feel? And why is Johanna here with Alexa? Johanna should have had the sense to stay home with the baby. I'm surprised you didn't invite Charlie Coscarelli. Maybe Liliana could sit on his lap and the two of them could kiss and make up."

"Well, I didn't invite Charlie; I'm not that stupid. I know that marriage is irreparable. Brendan says Johanna loves Alexa. People get over things, you know."

"You live in a dream world if you think Johanna and Alexa are ever going to be best buds. Johanna might be cool with it, but she would kiss a frog if it would make the poor little thing feel better. You should have asked Alexa before inviting Brendan and Johanna."

"Okay, people have grudges; but that's why I invited them. You and I have love to go around, so why not bring these others together? Maybe we can help them move beyond their feuds and squabbles. People can go from sad to happy if they let it happen."

"You overestimate people, Mother Teresa. I'm tired of

taking care of people so if you want to see me go from sad to happy, let's get this fiasco over. Okay?"

A minute later, Liam and Maria emerge from the bedroom like nothing has happened. "Let's try this again," Liam says. And as the sound of "Happy Birthday" fills the room, Maria wonders what's so happy about it. This time she blows the candles out—all thirty-five.

Kids make a party fun, and there's a houseful of them tonight. Alexa brought Cody. Dr. and Mrs. McDowell brought their recently recovered grandson, Morton. Johanna brought Sophia. Arianna and Danny Coscarelli brought their two girls, and Liliana brought her two boys. Tegan is in his element with all the kids around.

Mrs. Arioli is serving up the birthday cake when the doorbell rings. Miles Joyce barely makes it through the door before the crowd greets him in unison. "Father Miles!" That is, everybody except for one. Alexa runs and throws her arms around him. "Miles! I knew you'd come." Silence settles on the room. Alexa blushes and seems to suddenly remember herself. She turns to the crowd. "Okay, everybody listen up. I went on a spiritual retreat. I know some of you will laugh. Laugh all you want, but Miles will vouch for me. I can be extremely spiritual when I want to be. Miles has volunteered to be my spiritual advisor." The combination of birthday cake and alcohol can make anything sound plausible, and so the party goes on.

Soon Father Miles draws attention to give Maria her birthday blessing. "Maria, may you live as long as you want, and want for nothing as long as you live."

Maria gives a polite thank you and the crowd cheers. Now it's time for the birthday girl to open gifts. She unwraps a Yankee Candle from Alexa; a sweater from Mom and Dad; a wall hanging from Dr. and Mrs. McDowell; a few gift cards; and a bottle of body lotion from Tegan. "Just the kind Mommy loves," Maria assures him.

"Dad helped me pick it out." Tegan does a victory dance, and all the kids giggle.

Liam flashes Tegan a thumbs up. "It's you and me, buddy. Pals forever."

Liam hands Maria an envelope while everyone watches. She pulls out a gift certificate and howls. "A mud run! I've been dying to try a mud run. I hear they're crazy! Thank you, Liam."

"A mud run? Sounds dirty," scowls Mrs. Arioli.

Maria gives her the look of death. "Let it go, Mom. It's a race."

"Not just a race," Aiden chimes in. "It's a race where you crawl through mud pits, climb walls, swing on ropes, throw spears, jump over fire, and carry sand bags up hills. You name it, you do it—"

"—and at the finish line you get all the beer you want," Liam adds.

Leave it to Mrs. Arioli to throw water on the fire. "Should you be doing this at your age? What if you fall down in the fire?"

"You'd be surprised how many scrapes and bruises we see in the ER after these races," Brendan adds.

"I'd be more concerned about the infections," Dr.

McDowell says. "Who knows what bacteria lurk down in that mud?"

"I don't care what you say! I'm going to do the mud run. And nothing is going to stop me." Maria shoots an evil eye at the two doctors.

Then Mr. Arioli asks the group, "Would Jesus do a mud run?"

People laugh, but quickly cover their mouths when they realize the man is serious. There are a few shrugs and sidelong glances.

Father Miles Joyce rises to the occasion. "My friends, the real question is, 'Would Jesus win if he did a mud run?' I, for one, believe he would." Now that gets some laughs.

"Oh hell, I could beat Jesus," Aiden declares. Now everyone is laughing except Mr. and Mrs. Arioli. They don't approve of the priest's lifestyle, and although they would never say it, they are certain that Father Miles Joyce—priest or not—is going to hell.

"No reason to get excited," Liam intervenes. "The race is two months away, so we have plenty of time to train. I signed us both up; Maria and I are doing it together."

"Hey, we're doing it, too," says Aiden. "I mean, I'm doing it. Aoife was going to do the mud run, but . . ." He turns to Aoife and nods her forward.

"But I found out yesterday, I'm pregnant again. We decided to get back on the horse and give it another shot. Rationally, I know a mud run wouldn't hurt the baby, but I'm not taking any chances this time. We're sticking with the Irish naming tradition too. If he's a boy we're calling him Colin; if she's a girl we're naming her Orla."

Aoife pushes a polite smile towards Dr. and Mrs. McDowell. As the party resumes, Dr. and Mrs. McDowell make a point to go over and introduce themselves to Aoife.

"Please don't say anything more," Aoife says abruptly. "It was a painful chapter, but now it's over. I'm speaking for myself; Aiden needs more time. He seems to have taken this harder than me, so don't say anything to him. Tell Clare she is forgiven. I choose to live in the present and hold no grudges. Thank you." Aoife turns and disappears down the hallway towards the bathroom.

Mrs. McDowell takes a step toward the hall, but the doctor reaches out and stops her. "Best to let her go, Trudy. We said our peace, and she doesn't want to dredge any of this up. Talking about traumatic events only makes the feelings worse. Some things can't be changed."

"I know you're right; I just wish there was more we could do."

"Sometimes doing nothing *is* doing something—we're leaving her alone. I know it's hard for you, but it's the right thing to do."

Dr. McDowell takes a few steps and touches Liam on the arm. "Liam, could you and I have a word together?"

"Sure, doc, what's up?" Liam says, with a slight slur. The two men walk over to a quiet corner.

"Is Maria okay?" the doctor asks.

"If you're referring to that little incident over the picture, I'm sure she'll get over it. Is that what you're talking about?"

"Actually, I'm talking about work. Maria has been

the foundation of my practice for years now, but lately, she's making too many mistakes. Forgetting procedures, making inappropriate statements to the patients. It's like she's there, but she's not *really* there. She's going through the motions but her mind is on other things."

"I haven't seen anything like that," says Liam. "Is this serious? You're the doctor!"

"Well, I don't know what it is, but I'm worried about her. If she keeps this up, I'm going to have to start limiting her duties. She's always been a great nurse—the patients have never complained about her. But lately, I've had several complaints. I thought maybe you could shed some light on it."

"I have no clue what's going on, but I always see the best in Maria. I admit the picture incident tonight was a little over the top. Maybe it's a passing phase. Do you think she needs a physical exam?"

"It could be physical, but to me it looks like an emotional problem. Are the two of you getting along okay?"

"I'm surprised you ask that. Maria and I have never been better. We're solid here at home. There must be something in your office that's bothering her. This is a party. Can I suggest, respectfully, that you talk to Maria about what's bothering her at work. We don't have problems at home."

"Sorry to throw water on your party, Liam. If it continues at work, I'll talk to her about it," says Dr. McDowell.

Liam goes for another beer. Dr. McDowell goes to have a couple words with Trudy.

"We're taking off now," announces Dr. McDowell. "Happy birthday, Maria. See you tomorrow."

I Said "Ruining My Life"

After the party winds down, Liam locks the doors. He walks a crooked line back to turn off the lights, and tries to count how many beers he had. *Five? Maybe six. Wait, maybe seven.* He makes sure Tegan is asleep.

In the bedroom, he finds Maria propped up in bed, and as he puts on his pajamas, he says, "Nice party, but what was all that about?"

"My mom is getting on my nerves lately. I'm tired of her ruining my life."

"Okay, I admit your parents are annoyingly religious, but how is your mom running your life?"

"I said 'ruining my life,'" Maria sneers.

"Ruining your life? My God, why you would say that? I don't get it."

"Of course you don't get it. You had fun as a teenager. My parents never let me have fun. My mom picked out my clothes. They told me where I could go. They screened my friends. I had no fun whatsoever. You know why I became a nurse? Because my mother insisted that I was going to be a nurse; I never wanted to be a nurse. Now, half my life is over, and I've never been free to do what I want. I've never let loose. Never."

"Well," Liam responds slowly, "now you've got your chance. The mud run sounds wild and crazy, don't you think? Their website says, 'Get fit. Get focused. Get more sex!' That sounds wild and crazy to me."

Maria's eyes brighten. "The mud run is perfect, but don't get any ideas; you're not getting laid every night just because you do a mud run. And I don't care how fit you get."

"How about every other night?" He tickles her around the belly button.

"We'll see how fit you get!"

"Okay! We've got two months to train, and we're going to get wild and crazy. Let's have a blast." Liam drops his pajamas, crawls in with Maria, and they get the fun started then and there.

Trenbolone

The next morning Maria looks at her gifts sitting on the dresser. Body lotion. A wall hanging. A sweater and candle. *Old lady gifts—things you give your grandma.* Then it occurs to her: *Liam is right. The mud run is my chance to get wild and crazy. It's my last chance before I get old.* And she makes up her mind to go all in.

That very day, Maria starts training as if it's the only thing in the world that matters. She hangs a climbing rope from a tree and starts inching up and down like a caterpillar. She carves a broom handle into a spear and spends hour after hour hurling it at straw targets. She hauls a smelly tire out of a ditch and religiously lugs it up and down the mountains behind her house. She reads about a muscle-building supplement called Trenbolone—the article says it works miracles, and she orders a bottle off the internet.

In six short weeks, Maria develops the body of a freakishly fit sixteen-year-old boy, with bulging biceps, six-pack abs, thunder-thighs, a bubble butt, and puffed-out genitals. Practically overnight, Maria transforms herself into a stone-eyed, ass-kicking warrior—aggressive and powerful—just the attitude she needs to compete in the mud run.

She also gives herself a complete makeover. Her long, blond hair is replaced with a buzz cut on both sides and dreadlocks in the center—dreadlocks painted blue. The ass-kicking Maria has a nose-ring and four piercings in each ear. No more traditional dresses. She wears short shorts and halter tops from the girls' department at Target. She gets a new tattoo above her left breast: *Born for fun*.

It's like Tegan's traditional, tender mom moved out one day and a carousing teenage girl moved in the next. Liam doesn't know what to think. It's erotic and exotic but, on the other hand, what happened to the old Maria? He can't seem to say or do anything right for the new Maria. The night before the race, he walks into the bedroom to see Maria angrily sling her phone across the bed.

"What's bugging you now?"

"My parents saw my picture on Facebook and supposedly I'm a bad influence on Tegan. My dad says I look like a cross between a clown and a hooker. And my mother won't shut up about my tattoo. Apparently I'm not godly enough for them anymore."

"Well, who cares what they think? You do look different, though. I didn't know you were getting a tattoo. Where did you get it?"

"Where do you think I got it? Your brother did it. Aiden? Powerhouse Tattoos? Remember? Your brother with the thick, curly beard and his whole arm sleeved? Aiden is straight out of *Game of Thrones*. He's hot. Aoife must enjoy making babies with him!"

"That's enough, Maria. I don't want to hear it. He's my brother, so shut up. You look different and it's going to take people a while to get used to it."

"People better get used to it. I'm never going back to the way I was. From now on, I'm being true to myself. I'm having fun, and nobody is going to stop me."

"I'm not trying to stop you. I'm trying to be supportive, but don't start that shit about my brother again." Liam exhales. "Speaking of looks, I saw a receipt from the vision center on the counter. Are you getting new glasses?"

"I'm getting new contacts," she says. "You know, you've been lying to me for years. You say I look good in glasses. Well, I look terrible in glasses, and I'm getting contacts. You're a liar."

"Come on, Maria. I haven't been lying to you. I love you. To me, you're beautiful—with or without glasses. That's the truth, whether you like it or not."

But Maria doubles down. "You're a liar. I don't look good in glasses, and I'm getting contacts."

Liam stops and thinks. *What do you say when you tell a woman she's beautiful—and she calls you a liar?* "New contacts—awesome," is all he says. Then he crawls into bed and pretends to fall asleep.

Let the Games Begin

The next morning, Liam and Maria arrive at the race, and Liam gets his first lesson in mud-run culture: in mud running, attitude is everything. The gathered challengers are covered in badass tattoos, buzz-cuts, piercings, and face paint. There are women ready to crawl through the mud in their wedding dresses—a not-so-subtle F*#K YOU to their exes—and Special Forces wannabes on the prowl, dressed in commando outfits straight from the military surplus store. A few mud runners have taken their attitude to the next level and have branded themselves like cattle. Maria fits in perfectly.

Maria is a ticking time bomb, ready to explode with forces that have been boiling inside her for years. She ditches Liam and Aiden and shoves her way to the front of the crowd. Soon, horns begin to blare; storm clouds clash overhead; and hordes of buzzed, branded, dreadlocked, and tattooed runners move forward, growling and howling and pounding one another. The mud run has begun!

Maria shoots ahead of everyone and hurls herself over the first wall, shrieking like a banshee. But a funny thing happens on the way to the finish line: on to the scene steps Jaxon Ryder.

If you Google Jaxon Ryder, you find that he bills himself as a personal trainer and professional athlete. He travels the country doing mud runs and posts online photos of himself, tattooed, shirtless, and wearing tight shorts to show how fit he is. He scowls at the camera to let people know: *I'm bad.* Peel away the poser though, and you learn that Jaxon Ryder cleans tables in a restaurant. He has never come close to winning a race. He has never been on the podium. He has no sponsors. And as for being a personal trainer, he has no credentials except for the fact that he works out at the gym for thirty hours a week when he isn't cleaning tables.

Jaxon Ryder uses personal training and mud running to cheat on his wife, Hope, and his little girl, Justine. He lures women into personal training—he cops a feel here, grabs some ass there, and wraps his arms around them to show them how to move their bodies. He brushes his body against theirs, and if they don't object, he shoves his body against theirs to get them over the top. He motivates women by telling them they're hot. And as they work up an adrenaline-soaked sweat, he brags about what he'd do if he ever got them alone. Sometimes his female trainees go with him to mud runs; sometimes he meets them there. And he is always on the prowl for new trainees at the races. When the mud run is over, he drives home, kisses Hope and Justine, and the next morning he's back at work in the restaurant. Next weekend, he will hit the road again for his next mud run conquest.

Jaxon spots Maria running by herself in the middle of the race—she's a stray—and hobbles up to run alongside her. "I don't know if I'll be able to finish today. I fell off a wall last weekend and wrecked my knee," he grunts.

Maria responds like a tried and true mud runner: "Quit whining and get going!"

"Seriously, my knee isn't a hundred percent; I don't

think I can finish on my own."

Maria has never met Jaxon Ryder in her life, but she takes one look, sees something that looks fun, and jumps right in. "Let's run together and help each other!"

That was easy, Jaxon says to himself.

As Maria and Jaxon make their way along the course together, pushing each other over and under obstacles, things take a turn: this race is no longer about winning; it's about scoring. Maria is out for fun, and she has already decided that Jaxon Ryder is the one who's going to give it to her. Along with his ripped body and bad-boy attitude comes another appealing attribute: Jaxon is far younger than her—she's cranked up for a boy-toy!

Liam has told her a thousand times, "You look gorgeous," but that means nothing to Maria right now. If Jaxon would say "You look gorgeous" even once, Maria would tremble. Liam is been there, done that: Maria is craving shiny and new. She's getting out from under the thumb of Mom and Dad, and nothing is going to stop her.

Maria and Jaxon cross the finish line together, and he leads her past the beer-guzzling partiers to introduce her to Hope and Justine. "Maria is a dear friend," he tells Hope. "I couldn't have finished the race without her."

"Amazing!" says Hope.

"You have a beautiful family," Maria tells her.

"Thank you. I usually stay home with Justine, but today I wanted to bring her out to cheer for her dad."

Maria gives Hope a muddy peck on the cheek and whispers, "You must be an amazing wife and mother.

Jaxon is lucky to have you."

Then Maria gets down on one knee and smiles at Justine. "I'll bet you're proud of your daddy."

Justine wraps her arms around Maria's muddy neck. "Thank you for helping my daddy."

Maria gives Justine a muddy hug and says, "My pleasure; I'd help your daddy any time," with the subtlest of winks at Jaxon. Jaxon pinches himself again. *How easy can it get?*

You Want to What?

Beyond Jaxon's wife and kid, Maria has another problem: Liam. She fights her way through the crowd, and finds the two brothers partying with a marauding band of mud runners who appear to live by no rules but their own. "I really kicked some ass out there!" Maria yells, throwing her muddy arms around Liam's muddy neck. Maria, Liam, and Aiden swap kick-ass stories about mud, water, slipping, and sliding. Maria fails to mention Jaxon Ryder or his hurt knee. Not a word about Hope or baby Justine. *Lord, forgive us for the things we say—and the things we don't.*

Nasty brown goo oozes from every orifice of their bodies, so Liam and Maria take a well-deserved shower, bid Aiden good-bye, and start the drive back home to suburbia and middle-class parenthood. Along the way, Maria spots an adult toy store and makes an unusual request. "Stop! I want to shop for toys." Now, this may not be unusual for some couples, but Liam recalls only one time when Maria has ever visited an adult toy store, and on that occasion, her face turned red, she ran out the door, and he found her having a meltdown in the car.

"You want to what?"

"You heard me. I want to shop for sex toys. Doesn't the website say 'Get fit. Get focused. Get more sex?'"

Liam smiles. Maybe the new Maria is going to turn out okay, after all.

Inside the store, Maria is as happy as a girl who just got voted prom queen. She has forgotten what the word "embarrassed" means. She waltzes around trying on erotic masks, picking up vibrators and harnesses and waving them in Liam's face.

"Do you do demonstrations?" she asks the clerk.

"Not during store hours," she replies, barely looking up. She must get asked that pretty often.

What strikes Liam is the personality change; this is not the same woman he has been living with for the last twelve years. However, little does Liam know that he is not the object of Maria's new-found sexual excitement—today he is merely the chauffeur. As Maria parades through the adult toy store, she is jacking herself up for Jaxon Ryder.

A Name He Is Soon Going to Hate

The next morning, Liam wakes up feeling like a king. Maria has never been as sexually responsive as she was last night—she was insatiable. If he can get to where he feels good about the blue hair and bulging muscles, things are going to turn out fine between them.

Liam, however, is about to encounter a name he is soon

going to hate. To make matters worse, it is served up to him in a Facebook notification. In Maria's recent activity: a post on Jaxon Ryder's Facebook page.

Remember me? You looked hot yesterday.

Liam clicks on the man's name. Jaxon's profile is photo after photo of himself—head shaved, arms sleeved with tattoos, and a body that looks like he lives at the gym. At the end, there's a single photo of Hope and baby Justine.

Liam flies down the stairs and finds Maria sprawled on the sofa, her face buried in her phone.

"Who is Jaxon Ryder?"

"He's a guy I met at the race yesterday." She doesn't even look up.

"You can't be writing this shit on Facebook. Everyone can see it. It's humiliating. Who is he?"

She still doesn't take her eyes off the screen. "I told you, I met him at the mud run. But there's no need to worry— he wouldn't be interested in me. He can get all the pussy he wants."

"What in hell are you talking about? The guy is married and has a kid! Why would you say that?

"I'm saying it because it's true. He has the body of a god. He can have any girl he wants. He wouldn't be interested in me, so quit worrying about it."

This is the new Maria talking. Liam considers playing supportive husband one more time. *Maybe I should say, "Don't put yourself down. Of course Jaxon Ryder would be interested in you—any man would be."*

Liam can't do it anymore. He's tired of being the

supporting actor—he wants to be the leading man again. *Maybe I should tell Maria how I really feel. I should say, "I've had it with this bullshit, the buzz-cut and blue dreadlocks, the piercings, the badass attitude. This may be fun for you, but it's a nightmare for me." If I say that, Maria will say I'm trying to control her. She may even accuse me of abuse if I say it too forcefully.*

Slowly, he looks up at her: "I'm warning you. Get your act together. Go to counseling if you need it. You better start thinking about Tegan. If you want to destroy your life, that's up to you, but I'm not going to let you hurt Tegan with your adolescent games."

Maria reacts as predicted. "Here I am, finally having fun, and you're trying to stop me with threats and verbal abuse. You're a control freak. And I'm not going to put up with it."

In walks Tegan. "Dad, are we going hiking today? You promised."

"Sure. It's you and me, buddy. Pals forever."

So Liam, Tegan, and the dog take off into the mountains. Liam needs to clear his head. This thing with Maria isn't going away; it's only getting worse.

Employees Must Wash Their Hands

In fact, this thing with Maria is getting worse by the hour. Minutes after Liam heads off, Jaxon Ryder responds to Maria's Facebook message.

As if I could forget. Awesome to meet a dear friend yesterday. Maria responds.

Oh yeah.

This is a perfect day for Maria and Jaxon to cash in together. Liam and Tegan are out of the way, and Maria can justify her actions by telling herself that Liam yelled at her this morning. It's a good day for Jaxon, too. He's at work in the restaurant but has no qualms about texting at work.

Where do you work? Would you mind sending the answer on WhatsApp?

Maria doesn't think twice before moving to WhatsApp.

I'm a nurse. I work for Doctor McDowell.

For the next ninety minutes, Jaxon and Maria exchange sex messages and photos that culminate in Jaxon recording himself masturbating in the restroom at work. In full participation, Maria makes a masturbation video herself—right there on the sofa. And in the spirit of coming together, these two dear friends simultaneously push Send.

Jaxon gives a sigh of relief, and thinks, *I never dreamed it could be this easy.*

You're the One Who's Struggling

At lunchtime, Liam and Tegan roll in from the mountains to find Maria still Facebooking on the sofa, her feet propped up. "Mom, we didn't see anybody up in the mountains—not a soul up there," Tegan tells her.

"Thanks for the idea. That would be a good place for me to do my training," she tells him. "Now go take a shower and clean up for lunch."

Liam sits down with Maria on the sofa. "I did some

thinking this morning. I'm sorry I exploded. Maybe I haven't been a good listener lately. I know you're struggling with some things, and I was thinking maybe—"

"—I'm not struggling. You're the one who's struggling," Maria interrupts.

Liam pauses. There is a silence. "Anyway . . . I was thinking that maybe we should go to counseling together."

"Marriage counseling? Why?"

"Why? Obviously there's a lot of tension between us. We need to work things out."

"Look, I sent the guy an innocent Facebook message. Don't start chewing on the bone. Maybe we've got issues, but you're making a big deal out of it. We're not in a crisis."

"Maria, you aren't the same person you used to be. I'm worried about us. I want things to work between us. Why not give counseling a try?"

"Why can't you just let me be me? For once in my life I'm having fun, and you can't stand it. You're the one who is struggling, not me. So go to counseling if you want. But I'm not going. Now, can we chill for the rest of the day?"

The next afternoon, Maria hurries home from work—and this soon becomes a daily routine. On a typical day, Jaxon makes sex videos in the restaurant, but sometimes he does it from his bedroom, with Hope's clothes next to him and Justine's toys in the background. Maria is more creative. Taking a cue from Tegan, she starts doing training runs up in the mountains, where she takes off her clothes, rolls in the dirt, and takes photos of herself caked in mud. Soon she is sending Jaxon sex messages while she's at work in Dr. McDowell's office, and soon after that Maria and Jaxon begin hooking up at the Holiday Inn on the outskirts of Lovejoy. Maria pays for everything; Jaxon barely has gas money. Maria doesn't care. For once in her life, she's being herself. Having fun.

They Inject it in Cattle

One afternoon, Liam comes home early and walks into the bedroom. Three steps in, he stops dead in his tracks: Maria is perched on the bed in her bra and panties, a needle stuck in her thigh. "What are you doing?" he asks.

"What does it look like I'm doing? I'm taking my medication."

"What medication?" Liam grabs the vial off the bed, and quickly googles Trenbolone. "How long have you been taking this?"

"Four months—since I started training." Maria pulls the needle out, wipes blood off of her thigh, and grabs the vial out of his hand.

"This is an anabolic steroid."

"I'm a nurse; I don't need you to tell me what it is."

Liam reads the website to her: "Warning: Trenbolone may cause liver and kidney damage, heart-valve problems, infertility, and other medical conditions, including enlarged clitoris in women. Trenbolone is known to cause extreme aggression, severe mood swings, personality changes, and significant sex drive increases in women."

Maria snorts. "It doesn't say these things *will* happen; it only says they *could* happen. I'm monitoring my reactions to it."

"Who are you kidding? Your mood swings are constant. Your sex drive is off the charts. My God, they inject Trenbolone in cattle in the stockyards. Why didn't you tell me you were taking this!"

"Because I knew you wouldn't understand. And as usual, I was right."

"Maria, you've got to get off this shit. It's dangerous; it's destroying you."

"No way! I'm not going back to the way I was—a measly weasel trapped in a box. I'm free now. I'm going to keep doing mud runs. And you can't stop me!"

"Trenbolone is a class three drug. You could lose your nursing license if you get caught with it. Where did you get this? Are you getting drugs from Jaxon Ryder?"

"Why are you bringing him up again? He has nothing to do with this."

"He looks like the kind of guy who takes steroids."

"How would I know if he takes steroids? Lots of mud runners do—they work like magic. Anybody can get it on the internet. I don't even know Jaxon Ryder."

"Maria, you've got to be honest. If you are mixed up with Jaxon Ryder, you need to put it out there now."

"I promise you. I have nothing to do with him."

"Okay. This Trenbolone answers a lot of questions."

Do You Have Any Money?

Of course, Maria is lying, to herself and to Liam. Trenbolone is like candy to her, and her rebellious, adolescent attitude makes her feel like she can do anything. Text by text, video by video, hookup by hookup, Maria is giving control of her mind and body to Jaxon Ryder. Day by day, it gets harder to meaningfully distinguish between Jaxon and Maria—she agrees with him on everything.

One afternoon, in the afterglow of roughhouse sex, Jaxon asks Maria, "Do you have any money?"

"Like how much?"

"Like enough to take the summer off and travel around doing mud races. We could be professional athletes. We could make names for ourselves, and eventually get sponsors to pay us. I can get Hope to go along with it; that wouldn't be hard. If you play your cards right, you should be able to get that husband of yours to go along too."

A couple days later, Liam sits Maria down on the sofa, and confidently announces, "I've found help. There's a counselor in town who specializes in steroid abuse. I spoke with her at length, and I am sure she can help. She will meet with us next week, and I'm hoping you will give counseling a chance."

"That's impossible. I'm going away for the summer. I'm leaving next week. I'm calling it my summer of fun. You've been frustrated with me lately. I need time to sort things out. You need time for yourself too. Tegan will be fine here with you. And when I come back at the end of summer, things will be better for us."

Liam's jaw drops. He gapes at her, bewildered. "This is the steroids talking," he says. "Please don't do this. I'm begging you: *do not do this.*"

"Do what? I'm going away to do mud runs. What's wrong with that?"

"What about your job?"

"I quit my job yesterday. It's boring. The patients are sick all the time and Dr. McDowell says I can't wear my nose ring at work. So I quit. I'm not taking shit off anyone anymore. Those days are over."

"You quit your job, just like that, after nine years?"

"Yep. I've decided to become a professional athlete."

The second Liam hears the words "professional athlete," he feels it—this stinking mess has Jaxon Ryder written all over it. "What does 'professional athlete' mean? Would you get paid for mud running?"

"No, I wouldn't get paid at first. But if I get good at it, I might find a sponsor like Nike or Adidas. Who knows? I could become famous."

Liam's body stiffens. He feels his throat tighten. "You dreamed this up with Jaxon Ryder, didn't you?"

"This has nothing to do with Jaxon Ryder. It's about me being me."

Liam wants to grab Maria and shake her back, tell her to quit lying, that she is not going away on her summer of fun, that he is going to stop her. But he checks his anger: *What would happen to Tegan if I end up in jail?*

He takes a deep breath, and says, "Are you asking my permission?"

"I just want to know if you will go along with it."

Liam swallows hard and looks his wife hard in the eyes. "I'm taking the high road on this. I don't want you to go, and I'm surprised you would leave Tegan. I want you to stay here, to get off the steroids, and to help me put our lives back together. But you're not a child and I'm not your father. Whether you go or not is your decision—not mine. So go if you want. But if I find out that you're running with Jaxon Ryder, I will not take you back at the end of the summer. I promise you that—you run off with him and I will not take you back."

Maria rolls her eyes. "Why are you against everything I do?"

"This isn't about you. Or me. It's about us. It's about Tegan. If you run off with Jaxon Ryder and I take you back I will never be able to look my son in the eye again. What kind of example would I be? You wouldn't respect me if I took you back, and I wouldn't respect myself. I'm not living the rest of my life without respect for myself. So I'm taking the high road: it's your decision. So you better think about what you're doing."

Everything I Need to Know

The only thing Maria takes away from this conversation is that Liam isn't going to stop her. He basically just gave her permission to go. So she starts counting down the days until her summer of fun begins, thinking about how it will feel to be free: free to be herself, free to go anywhere she wants, free to do anything she wants.

Liam sits on their bed, eyes glazed. He still loves Maria, but not the woman she's become. He can feel Jaxon Ryder breathing on his neck, lurking in the shadows. But, where is the confirmation? *Do I really know this or am I crazy?*

Am I a control freak? How can I really know?

Then it occurs to him: *Everything I need to know is in her phone.*

So Liam makes up his mind that he's going to hack into Maria's phone. One problem: Maria guards her phone like it's a heap of gold. It never leaves her sight; she carries it from room to room, including the bathroom. Even if Liam could get his hands on it, he doesn't know the passcode. He's an engineer, so he does the math. There are millions of combinations. Even the FBI couldn't crack it. Maybe it's part of her social security number? Her phone number? A credit card? Her birthdate? Over the next few days, Liam focuses on nothing but combinations of numbers. And he's running out of time.

Then, three days before Maria is set to leave on her summer of fun, Liam gets a break. It's two in the morning, and as he lies in the dark next to Maria, her phone pings. It wakes him up, but he doesn't make a sound. Doesn't turn over. One eye eases open. Maria pulls the dimly lit screen to her face and puts in the passcode. Bingo! 2178— the last four digits of her social security number. Maria shoots a quick reply and goes back to sleep.

Still, the problem seems insurmountable. What good is the passcode if Maria's phone is surgically implanted in her hand? She never lays it down, and the more she guards it, the more he feels the need to see what's in it. In twenty-four hours, Maria is getting in her car to leave for her summer of fun, and when she does, Liam will lose the only woman he has ever loved. He can't let that happen.

We Don't Believe in Divorce

Liam turns to Maria's sister. Maybe Alexa can talk some sense into her. This is risky business; Alexa doesn't want to hear about their personal problems. It could all backfire. He closes his office door, and tells Siri, "Call Alexa."

"Hey, Brother-in-Law. Is Maria getting ready for her summer of fun?"

"Well, that's what I called to talk about. Alexa, is anyone in your family worried about Maria? I mean, she quit her job, she's bulked up, and she has blue dreadlocks and a ring in her nose. Is anyone concerned?"

"Not that I know of. My parents can't stand her hair or clothes, but they never like anything. We're used to that. To me, the only thing that has changed is Maria is happy. That's all that matters to me."

"Alexa, you don't get muscles like that just by working out. She's using steroids—steroids they give to cattle, for God's sake. This doesn't worry anyone?"

"I can't imagine my big sister putting anything in her body that's bad for her. After all, she's a nurse. All I care about is that mud running has changed her life, and I have to say, it's pretty big of you to let her go away for the summer. Most husbands wouldn't let their wives go like this. You're good with Tegan, so it should turn out okay."

"That's just it. I didn't give her permission. I told her that if she goes, she's not coming back home."

"Not coming back home? What do you mean?"

"I mean, I love her, but I'm not about to let her go off and cheat on me only to take her back at the end of the summer. Love doesn't work that way, at least not in my book."

"Cheat on you? You're starting to sound like a typical man now. What makes you think she is going to cheat on you?"

"I suspect she's already cheating on me. With this guy she met at the mud run."

"You mean Jaxon Ryder?"

"Exactly. How do you know his name?"

"I saw what Maria put on his Facebook page. Everybody saw it. To me, it was totally innocent, but some people are surprised you put up with it."

"Put up with it? What am I supposed to do about it? She doesn't ask my permission; she's her own person. And by the way, her posts aren't innocent. I've got a hunch that this Jaxon Ryder is what prompted her summer of fun."

"I don't think Maria would cheat on you with Jaxon Ryder. I doubt he'd be interested in her. With a body like his, he can have any woman he wants. I might stand in line for a piece of it myself."

"Very funny." Liam grits his teeth.

"Hey, it's the way men talk about women—what goes around, as they say. You know, our family doesn't believe in divorce, if that's what you mean by her not coming home."

"I don't want a divorce; I love Maria—at least, the old Maria. But I have my limits. Can you talk some sense into her? She doesn't listen to me. Do it for Tegan. Maria may be his mother, but I'm not going to let her hurt him. And you don't need to discuss this with your mom and dad;

they wouldn't understand."

"Okay, I'll talk to Maria this afternoon. Bye."

Liam gives a sigh of relief, and tries to get some work done before he heads home. In his heart of hearts, he feels sure Maria will call off the trip. *We're a perfect family. Sure, every couple has problems, but you persevere. You talk things out. Surely we can weather a little mid-life crisis.*

Three hours later, Liam pulls into the driveway. Alexa's car is out front. Maria's mom and dad are waiting for him in the living room, along with Alexa—sitting stiff as corpses. Maria and Tegan are nowhere to be seen.

"We talked to Maria—all three of us," says Alexa. "She swears she met Jaxon Ryder at the mud run and hasn't seen him since. We believe her."

"I may not like Maria's latest hair style," says Mrs. Arioli, "but she's my daughter, and will always be. Despite our disagreements, I will always take her side. You will never turn us against her. Nothing can separate us from the love of God and the love we have as a family."

"Liam, do you consider yourself a Christian?" Mr. Arioli chimes in.

"What kind of question is that? Of course I do."

"Then you better read First Corinthians, chapter thirteen. It tells us what love is, and you won't read the word 'divorce' in there. If you love my daughter, go to church and stop threatening to divorce her."

Liam clenches his jaw. "Where are Maria and Tegan?"

"We sent them to dinner, so we could talk to you," Alexa

says. "I'm taking Tegan home to play with Cody for the evening. This will give you and Maria some time to kiss and make up. I'll bring Tegan back later."

"Thanks for the help," Liam snaps at Alexa, as he abruptly escorts them to the door.

"You need to lay off my sister," Alexa snarls.

Liam locks the door behind them.

Give Me the Phone

It isn't long before Maria returns and the two of them square off in the living room, face to face, standing no more than six feet apart. Liam's eyes lock on Maria's phone, then to her face, then back to the phone. It's right there in her hand—only six feet away.

Maria lashes out. "I don't appreciate you sharing our personal business with my family, especially when half of it isn't true. I can't believe you would accuse me—"

"Let me see your phone," he demands.

"Why?"

"Why not? If you have nothing to hide?"

Maria juggles the phone up and down in front of him, taunting him. "There—you see it. Does that make you happy?"

"I said give me the phone!"

Maria has to think quick. *He has no right to go through my phone—that's phone stalking. Then again, he doesn't know the passcode, so why not play along?*

She tosses him the phone. "Play with it all you want," she laughs.

In an instant, Liam taps in 2178. Maria is paralyzed as Liam dives into her netherworld. He opens WhatsApp and after a few moments, his face drains of color. Reading her messages is like visiting a war zone: messages like new offensives, evidence of subterfuge—the ruins of a relationship he once treasured, all graphic and raw. Maria has been sexting with Jaxon Ryder practically every day for five months—and has deleted none of it. Every video, every photo, every sexy turn-on confirms what Liam has been feeling for months.

In this moment, Liam feels disgusted . . .but he also feels pity. He hands the phone back to Maria, and politely says, "Thank you."

"I can explain," Maria begs.

"You've been sleeping with Jaxon Ryder for months. And lying about it. And you can explain it? Hit me with your best shot. Please explain."

"Okay. You know. I've given myself permission to go wild and crazy this summer. I don't want any responsibilities. I just want to have fun. I'm doing what I never got to do as a teenager. I'm thirty-five; it's my last chance."

"Humiliating. For both of us. But continue."

"Don't take it personally, Liam. It has nothing to do with you; I'm just having fun. You're good in bed; you're the best. You really are. It's just that right now I need more. That's the only way I can explain it."

"What happened to your morals? This guy has a wife and kid. What's going to happen when his wife finds out?"

"Everyone has their own morals—I have mine, you

have yours, she has hers. If she finds out, that's her problem, not mine. I know a lot of people wouldn't agree with the sex that goes on at mud runs, but sex is part of the deal. You read the website: Get fit. Get focused. Get more sex. It's why people get into mud running in the first place."

Liam can't help but wonder. *Is this Jaxon Ryder talking? Is it Trenbolone? Is it the rebellious teenager telling her parents where to go and how to get there?* All Liam knows is that this is not the Maria he loved. He doesn't even like the woman he is talking to.

"These steroids are not only wrecking your body, they're screwing up your head."

Maria's eyes turn to glass. She cocks her fist and punches Liam in the chest. "You're a control freak," she shouts. "I've been talking to Jaxon, and he thinks you and I need a break from one another."

Liam steps backwards. "Excuse me, Maria, if I don't have a deep conversation with you about Jaxon Ryder's marital advice. He's despicable. I agree with him on one point, though. You and I need a break—we're breaking up."

"As usual, you aren't listening. I didn't say that I want us to break up. I said that we need a break—for the summer. That's the plan. I don't want to break up with you."

"Hmmm," says Liam. "I know you don't want to break up with me—but you just did." Liam turns on his heel, marches into the guest bedroom, and locks the door. Later that evening, after Tegan comes home from Aunt Alexa's, Liam tucks him in and together they say their prayers.

That Girl is Dead

The next morning, Maria gets up at the crack of dawn and loads her car. Liam is up early too. He sits in the living room and studies the family photo that Alexa took on Maria's birthday—a mere five months ago. The three of them look happy in the picture—Maria, Tegan, and him. He recreates every detail of that evening, searches for clues of what was to come, and tries to understand why he didn't see it coming. Maria had said, "I look terrible," but in hindsight, he understands what she really meant: "I feel terrible."

The car is packed, and as Maria bounces past the living room, Liam snaps out of his trance. Something in him still won't give up hope.

"Maria," he says, "Look." He holds up the photo. "This is our family, Maria."

Maria looks at it with a blank face, glassy-eyed, as if she doesn't even recognize the people in the frame. "That girl is dead," she pronounces as she points at herself in the photo.

At that moment, Liam knows the truth. *The Maria he loved is dead. And so is his perfect family.*

Maria tiptoes into Tegan's room and kisses him on the forehead, being careful not to wake him up. "Take care of my little boy," she instructs Liam. Then she hugs Liam. "Goodbye." She gets in her car, and backs out of the drive. As Maria drives away for her summer of fun, Liam takes out his phone and sends her a message:

Have fun.

It's all he has left in him. He goes inside, sits on the sofa, and thinks about what he will say to Tegan when he wakes up. Maybe he will just say, "It's you and me, buddy. Pals forever."

HOME TRUTHS

Maria

Bless me, Father, for I have sinned. I can only guess how long since my last confession—a few years maybe?—but a lot has happened lately. . . Wait a minute. If we're doing this face-to-face, am I supposed to call you Father or Miles?

Miles

You're supposed to call me "Father," and I'm supposed to call you "my child." That's the traditional way: it's a sign of deference and humility. Nowadays, we're more casual. Of course, we both know I'm not your Father, and you're not a child. So let's not get hung up on formalities and hocus-pocus. What's important is what we say, not how we say it. What brings you to confession after all these years?

Maria

What brings me to confession? That's hard to say, Miles. You know that my sister Alexa plunged into spirituality after she had Cody, and then she went on your spiritual retreat. She is absolutely convinced that confession would do me a world of good, and has been all over me about it since my summer of fun. Even by sister standards, Alexa can be a real pain in the ass once she gets an idea in her head. So I'm here.

Miles

What Alexa wants, Alexa gets. I know. But this is about you, not Alexa.

Maria

So why am I here? Obviously I'm here to seek forgiveness. But I can't say exactly what for. You know about my summer of fun—

Miles

Maria, half of Lovejoy knows about it, thanks to your posts on Facebook.

Maria

Here's the way I look at it. I think I am pretty brave for going out on my own and kicking ass, as they say. I had a fabulous summer; I've never had so much fun in my life. Most women would pin a badge of courage on me for breaking out of the mold—they only wish they had the balls to do it themselves. So I'm not here to apologize for breaking free. I'm here because I pretty much committed every sin in the book. I ran away. Lost my mind on drugs. Cheated on my husband many times with many people. And lied about it, of course. I didn't honor my father or my mother by any stretch of the imagination. I left my child for the summer; although, in my own defense, I knew Liam would take good care of Tegan. I'm sure I committed more, but is there a blanket sin to cover the entire list? Something like going to the dark side?

Miles

You don't need to list every rule you've broken. Life is never as simple as following rules or breaking them. I'd rather focus on understanding your attitudes and intentions. It's not up to me to judge whether you let God down or let yourself down. You can decide that for yourself. Do you have any regrets about your summer adventure?

Maria

I regret a few things. I never found a sponsor, so I ran out of money. That was hard. At first, Jaxon Ryder, my companion, was like a counselor to me. But when I ran out of money, he ran off with a woman from Iowa or Nebraska—somewhere in the Midwest. That turned out to be a relief because we weren't getting along anyway. After that, I hooked up with a girl from Texas, and we were kind of a modern-day Thelma and Louise. We went for broke, nothing but fun, and I've never felt so high.

Miles

Jaxon Ryder, a counselor? You have a strange way of picking out counselors. Were you surprised he dumped you?

Maria

I don't care about Jaxon Ryder. And no, it didn't surprise me. He used me. I used him. Eventually we outgrew one another. He gave me the strength to pull this off, but he turned out to be a leech, so he had to go. I wasn't about to let him hold me back. Do you know Jaxon?

Miles

As I said, half of Lovejoy knows who Jaxon Ryder is, thanks to you and Facebook. You didn't exactly try to hide what you were up to over the summer. Perhaps you should add oversharing to your list of transgressions. That's a joke, by the way—but in the future you may want to rethink what you put out on social media. Anyway, back to your regrets.

Maria

My real regrets started when I came back at the end of summer. I thought that I would have my summer of fun, and then Liam would take me back when I came home. Looking back, I know it sounds crazy, but I really did believe that. I thought he would stick by me, but he was cold as a rock when I came back. He says he will always love me, but he won't even discuss getting back together. He has filed for divorce. Of course, being the optimist I am, I've been holding out hope that he might change his mind. Yesterday, I realized it's out of the question. He isn't going to take me back.

Miles

Even if Liam does love you, which I think he does, asking him to forgive is probably asking too much. He isn't about to give up his self-respect—not to anyone, not even you. A loving parent will forgive practically anything, but Liam isn't your father.

Maria

I'm not looking for a father, Miles. Liam said that himself: *I'm not your father.* You guys get into the father thing a little too much. I have a father, and none of this has anything to do with him. I'm doing fine on my own. I don't need a man to take care of me.

Miles

I think it has everything to do with your father. The Urge dug its claws into you pretty deep, Maria. You know what I'm talking about, right?

Maria

You're a deep thinker, Miles. I understand about half of what you say.

Miles

Okay, here it is. I'm talking about the urge to quit, to say "To hell with it," and run away. No responsibilities. No rules. No regrets. You just say, "I don't care" and let the chips fall where they may. I could sense your restlessness that night at your birthday party. It's nothing to be ashamed of. Everyone feels the Urge at one time or another. It creeps up on us when we least expect it. Maybe you lose someone or something you love and it leaves a hole in your heart. Suddenly, you're desperate to fill that hole with anything that will ease the pain. Drugs. Gambling. Sex. Porn every day. And you don't care about the consequences.

Say some guy gets passed over for a promotion and a low rage starts to smolder inside him. Then one day that rage bursts into flames, spreads like a forest fire, and burns down his house. Maybe all the houses around it. But he doesn't care that everything is torched, because, well . . . because he just doesn't care.

Or maybe one day you look in a mirror, and remember that guys used to look you up and down but now they look past you like you aren't even there. That's when the Urge digs in. You feel desperate; you have to do something—now.

The Urge usually starts with a throbbing sensation in the body. You feel that throb, and suddenly you feel like everyone around you is juiced up, sexed up, and having a blast—at a party you weren't even invited to. You crave a piece of the action. You need it, and you don't care who gets hurt in the process.

Maria

What would a priest know about throbbing in the body? You've taken the vow of celibacy. You're not allowed to throb, are you?

Miles

Priests are human, and we throb too. You may not know it, but there are days when I am tempted to tell everyone to go to hell, throw my priest collar in the trashcan, and head to Vegas. You think nurses are overwhelmed with responsibilities? Try working for God. Priests are supposed to care for everyone. All the time. It's one hell of a job, believe me. I'm not defending evil priests, but we carry a heavy burden, and we're humans first, priests second. Anyone who cares will feel the Urge from time to time, and the more you care, the more you're going to feel it.

Maria

Okay, we're getting somewhere now. You understand what I was going through. The Urge. I felt like middle age was breathing down my neck and life was passing me by. You know how old-fashioned my parents are. All my life, I felt trapped. Like I couldn't breathe. To my parents, taking care of people—husbands, boyfriends, parents, kids, sick, disabled, frail people—taking care of everyone, really, is the only thing that women are supposed to do. It seems like the only person a woman isn't supposed to take care of is herself. Thank you, Mom and Dad. Here I am, a nurse: something I never wanted to be. I'm an unemployed nurse at the moment, but a nurse just the same.

When I first met Liam, I absolutely loved the way he made me feel. He was my escape. Liam let me be me. He didn't pontificate and point the finger. But as time went by, I realized that Liam had his own expectations for me.

He has his act together; he's sure-footed and confident. And soon enough, I was living in his shadow, striving to live up to his standards. He was *the man* and I was *his loving, devoted wife.* So I ended up feeling like I did with my parents—like I had to get out from under his shadow.

Then Tegan came along, and my life belonged to him. You know the drill: you have to show everyone what a great mother you are. So I put my kid first, like most mothers do. And I put my life on hold, under the illusion that if I made Liam and Tegan happy, then I would be happy. *Be a caring daughter, caring wife, and caring mother, and someday you'll get to feel good.* That's the promise for women, right? Well, it didn't work out that way for me. I had been taking care of others all my life, and I was miserable.

Sure, Liam and Tegan loved me, but I didn't know who "me" was. Then one day (you sensed it right, Miles), on my thirty-fifth birthday to be exact, it hit me—the Urge, as you call it. It was like a switch flipped off, and suddenly I didn't care about anyone anymore. Not even Tegan. So I ran away to go find myself. I guess that's a sin—for women.

<u>Miles</u>
Everyone is dying to know: Did you find yourself, Maria? And do you like what you found?

<u>Maria</u>
I love myself now. I love myself as much as I love Tegan— and for the record, I do love him dearly. I feel alive in a way I didn't before. You've known me a long time, Miles. I

was a simple, timid church girl—one of millions. Now I'm one of a kind. I'm the butterfly who emerged out of her dingy, gray cocoon. Sure, I paid a price for my confidence, which makes it all the more priceless to me. People can judge me all they want—they can say I'm a bad daughter, bad mother, and bad wife. I don't care.

Miles

Relax, Maria. I don't judge you for wanting to be free. Everyone wants to be free. They might not go about it the way you did, but that's what freedom is—living on your own terms, whether anyone else agrees with you or not. You might have made the mistake of believing that painting your hair, adding some piercings and a tattoo would change who you are. You do look different, but it doesn't change you on the inside.

To me, your motives sound pure and noble, and you're right: if you were a man, you would probably be hailed as a hero—a tarnished hero perhaps, but a hero just the same. All heroes have flaws—even in the Bible. It seems that looking for yourself and looking for trouble seem to go hand-in-hand, and slaying giants often involves slaying a lot of innocent people along the way. Of course, you don't have to slay a giant to figure out who you are.

So I don't judge you, and neither does God. God is a loving parent, and will forgive anything. You can rest assured that God has already forgiven you. I hope that knowledge comforts you. But I figure God is probably the least of your problems right now.

Maria

You're a priest, Miles. Isn't confession about getting right with God?

Miles

Well, it would be nice if all we had to deal with was God, but here on Earth, we have to deal with people—people and shit—our own shit, those we shit on, and those who shit on us. Confession is for sorting out the shit, and we clean up what we can as best we can. God forgives us, but confession doesn't erase the problems.

Maria

If you're suggesting I screwed Liam, I couldn't agree more. Liam didn't deserve this. I know I hurt him—him and our son. And other people. But I didn't plan this. I never saw it coming. People can hate me if they want, but nobody could hate me as much as I hated myself before I ran away. I broke the rules, I admit that, but I don't care what anyone thinks.

Miles

There's the Urge talking again. "I don't care." The three most dangerous words in the human language. Maria, wrong isn't wrong because we break a rule. Wrong is wrong when we steal our happiness from someone who cares about us and is counting on us. When it comes to forgiveness, I figure you have a couple of people to think about.

<u>Maria</u>

Obviously you think Liam is one of them.

<u>Miles</u>

I'm not worried about Liam. He's wounded, but he's a big boy and I'm sure he'll come out of this with his dignity intact—and he'll be far smarter. But would it kill you to tell him you're sorry?

<u>Maria</u>

I've thought about it. But I don't know how he'd take it.

<u>Miles</u>

How he takes it is up to him. If he shows his ass, that's his problem, not yours. I'm asking you to apologize for your sake, not his. You want to be free, right?

<u>Maria</u>

That's what this is all about.

<u>Miles</u>

Then you take responsibility. And when the time is right, say, "I'm sorry" and mean it. Don't worry about how he reacts; you're doing it for yourself. You'll feel a load lifted, trust me.

<u>Maria</u>

And the other person? You said there are two.

Miles

The other one. Okay, I've listened to your story; now let me tell you mine. You see, Maria, when I preside over Mass, I am up in the front, and everyone watches everything I do. But what people in the pews don't realize is that I'm watching them. And I see everything—every smile, every sigh, every scowl. I know who sings and who doesn't, who says the prayers and who stares into space. I can tell which couples had a fun Saturday night and those who had an argument. If somebody farts in church, I usually know who it was. In the pews, every face tells a story.

Maria

I'll have to remember that: Father Miles Joyce, the Creeper.

Miles

Maria, I can't tell you how many times over the summer I watched Tegan sitting next to his father crying his eyes out. It went on Sunday after Sunday. It broke my heart watching your little boy cry. If it makes you feel better, Liam seemed to do a good job of comforting him, but clearly Tegan was hurting. Tegan is a little boy, and kids usually don't get a voice in these matters, but I wouldn't be much of a priest if I didn't speak up on his behalf: I think it's terrible the way your parents boxed you in as a child, but it's not Tegan's fault that his mother had strict parents. I'm not trying to lay a guilt trip on you; mothers can't be everything their children need. I understand you had to seek your own freedom, but I have to tell you what

I personally witnessed. Your summer of fun wasn't much fun for your son. I don't know where the line between being a fulfilled woman and a good mother is—so don't ask me for the answers here.

Maria

Home truths, Father.

Miles

Home truths?

Maria

Home truths. It's an Irish expression. Liam and his brothers use it—truth that hits home. Miles, I love Tegan. Apart from my bravado, I love him more than I love myself. Maybe trying to be a giant-slayer hardened my heart, but you can't slay giants with a soft heart. I never meant to hurt Tegan or steal his happiness. Is Tegan the other person? Do you think I should ask Tegan to forgive me?

Miles

No, my child. Don't ask Tegan to forgive you; he's just a kid. The other person you need to forgive is the hardest person in the world to forgive: Yourself. I'm asking you to cut yourself some slack. Last summer, you gave in to the Urge: it happens to the best of us. So go easy on yourself, and don't start telling yourself what a bad mother you are, because from here on out Tegan is counting on you to fight the Urge. He needs you now more than ever, and "I don't care" isn't going to cut it with him. If you take good care of yourself, caring for Tegan will follow suit. Maybe you can just slay giants on the weekends or something.

Maria

Father, I am truly sorry, and if this is my moment of truth, then I have another confession to make. I haven't told anyone this, not even Alexa; I can barely face it myself. But yesterday I found out I'm pregnant. So now this is about more than just Tegan.

Miles

My child, should I assume that Liam is not the father of this baby?

Maria

I could make up a story, Miles, but . . . I don't know who the father is. It's not Liam. I was in party mode all summer. Someone told me I wouldn't get pregnant if I was taking steroids. I wasn't taking my birth control pills regularly; I'd skip a day here and there. I've narrowed it down to three guys. I don't think it matters; I am keeping this baby. And that's how I know Liam will never take me back.

Miles

I am happy for you, Maria, but troubled too. Didn't anyone teach you and your sister how to use birth control? Do I need to remind you that you're a nurse?

Maria

That's a dumb question, Miles. You know my mom and dad—straight-laced Catholics. Birth control and Catholics don't mix, remember? Need I remind you that you're a priest? Get back in line or you'll be the one going to confession. I can see the headline now: Creepy Father Miles Joyce Recommends Birth Control.

Miles

Point taken, Maria.

Maria

Look, I have to find a job fast, and I've got an interview in two hours. So I have to go. Presuming I'm not leaving you with the urge to run away to Vegas, can we talk about this again? Soon?

Miles

I'll hear your confession anytime, Maria. Just promise me you'll get off the steroids if you haven't already. Clean up your look before you go for the interview. You and Alexa keep things interesting around here; no one can dispute that. Of course, that's me speaking, not God.

Maria

It's who we are, Miles. The Arioli sisters—we shoot 'em up, slay giants, and cover one another's backs.

Miles

Just remember: I'm on your side, so don't go shooting at me. I don't know if that's God speaking or me.

Maria

Isn't this where you're supposed to say, "Go forth my child, and sin no more?"

Miles

Here's my blessing: May God the loving parent forgive all your shortcomings, spoken and unspoken. May you always forgive yourself and find peace in your heart. May you forgive others and bring peace to the hearts of those who suffer on your account. May you fly like the butterfly you are, and slay the giants that come your way, while always being careful with the hearts of those who love and count on you. May you find happiness with Tegan and your new baby, and may your love transform you into the caring person you are meant to be. Amen.

LOVE YOU CAN COUNT ON

Convivendo

Antonio bought a dark Alfani jacket and a crisp Hugo Boss dress shirt for the occasion. He made reservations at Cucina Emil, the only authentic Italian restaurant in Lovejoy—they make the pasta right on the premises there. It's hard to get a table on a Saturday night, but Tony managed it. When he and Madalena arrived, the *maître'd'* escorted them directly to their table, and Tony ordered a bottle of Rosso del Conte, an exquisite wine from the Italian heartland. He even pronounced the name perfectly. Biagio Antonacci was singing "Convivendo" on the sound system, and Madi knew that they might be listening to this same music if they were sipping wine on a veranda in Tuscany. She was savoring the magic and knew that when the climax of the evening came, there was no way she was going to say no.

Halfway through their second bottle of Rosso del Conte, Tony turned to Madi and delicately placed his left hand on her thigh and his right hand on her cheek. The mood was electric, and Madi felt like she was about to explode. He looked deep into her eyes, lowered his voice, and said:

"I have a proposition to make. I'd like you to marry me. Before you give your answer, though, I want to throw out an idea. I've done my homework, and an average engagement ring runs around five thousand dollars. Now, you're above average, so I planned to spend seven thousand. But instead of wasting that money on an ornament that will plummet in value the minute I slip it on your finger, I propose that we take the seven thousand and invest it in our future. In fifteen years, it could be worth twelve thousand, adjusting for inflation."

At first, Madi thought she was hearing things; maybe she'd had too much to drink. "Can you repeat that?" But when Tony started through his proposal again, matching it word for word as though he had it memorized, she stopped him mid-sentence and pushed his hands away.

"No."

"No what? No, meaning you want the diamond? Or no, meaning you don't want to marry me?"

"Just no," she growled. Suddenly all Madi could see around her were plates smeared with half-eaten, saliva-laced food; people snorting; kids whining; and dishes clanking. The music sounded crass and mocking—it belonged back in Italy where people actually know what "Convivendo" means. "Right now, I don't even want to be here with you." She excused herself and hoofed it out the door. An icy breeze hit her and her body bristled, the cold seeming to settle in her bones. Wiping the tears from her phone, she texted her friends for a ride home.

Tony sat alone and calculated the cost of a single ounce

of Rossa del Conte, then asked the waiter, "Can I re-cork the bottle and take it home?"

"That's not only illegal, but pretty damn tacky," came the reply.

So Tony tipped back his head and chugged the bottle, while the other diners pretended not to have seen what had just happened at the table in the corner. He paid the bill and left, all the while wondering why Madi couldn't understand that if you wanted to waste money, you might as well just throw it in the trashcan.

Madi caught a ride home with her girlfriends, who were pretty wasted and wouldn't stop laughing about Tony's lame proposal. As inebriated girlfriends will do, they didn't hold anything back. "You're too sweet for your own good. Why didn't you move Tony to the friend category a long time ago? He's a nice guy, but more like a brother—definitely not marriage material," one scolded her.

"If Tony is so worried about waste, why doesn't he worry about the year of your life you wasted on him?" squawked another.

As they pulled up in front of Madi's apartment, a third gave some parting advice. "Go lick your wounds, and when you've cried it out, pull out your fuck-me pumps, and we'll spread the word that you're back on the market. You'll be partying hearty in no time, and Tony will be a distant memory. Now, promise you won't download "Convivendo" and spend the night crying in Italian!"

Everyone laughed but Madi. "You don't have to worry about me." But the poor girl went inside, devoured two mega-size chocolate bars, and ended up crying herself to sleep, "Convivendo" on the loop.

He's Just an Accountant

The next morning, Madi woke up with a hangover to crush all hangovers. She fixed a cup of coffee and started looking for ways to take the sting out of last night's fiasco. In the new light of day, the buzz from the wine fading, the incident didn't feel quite as fatal.

Tony didn't intend to hurt me; it's just the way he is. Okay, so he's not sentimental, but he is reliable. He's not flashy, but he's steady for the long haul. He's not sexy; he's like that cozy comforter on my bed. He isn't mean. Or demanding. Not a player, stoner, or alcoholic. He's just an accountant. He loves to count. He wastes nothing and keeps track of everything. He always has a plan B. He fantasizes about financial freedom and gets off on calculating returns on investments the same way some guys might be attracted to a cute smile or a nice ass. Nobody would call on Tony to fight off marauders or defend the gates, but he is a wild man when it comes to having his finances in order. He can be boring, but there's more to life than romance. I don't care what my friends say; he is husband material. He will be faithful, a good provider, and an involved father.

As Madi sat considering all this, she realized that the botched marriage proposal was Tony's attempt to show off; he was trying to show that he has what it takes to be a good provider. Despite everything, Madi smiled. She wasn't going to cut Tony loose over an ill-conceived marriage proposal. She knew she loved the man and everything he stood for.

Tony doesn't understand the difference between a marriage proposal and a business plan. So Madi hatched a plan to strike a deal of her own and have some fun with Tony at the same time. *This is gonna be good.* She texted Tony to meet her at the Coffee Bean Café in three hours.

It's the least you can do, after what you pulled last night.

She jumped in the shower to get squeaky clean, meticulously put on her make up, and rifled through the closet to find the perfect outfit to drive him crazy.

Three hours later, Tony walked into the Coffee Bean Café, to find Madi waiting at a table in the corner. It was a Sunday afternoon, but she was wearing a navy-blue skirt and jacket, white satin top, and dark heels. Her hair was pulled back in a style straight out of *Fortune* magazine. Her eyes were circled by smart, no-nonsense, dark-framed glasses. "Sit down," she gestured. "Can I get you something to drink?"

"I've had enough to drink," Tony grumbled.

"Let's get down to business. I've considered your proposal, and while the basic concept has merits, there are aspects of the deal that need further clarification. I'm sure that you want any contract we put together to further your goals as well as mine. Don't you agree?"

"What contract?"

She slid a sheet of paper across the table. "Here is my counterproposal. Read it and, if you agree to the terms, sign it. This contract will be binding, so if you have questions, let's get them answered to avoid confusion at a later time. I hope you find the terms satisfactory and that we can reach a meeting of the minds today, while the offer is still on the table."

Tony picked up the contract.

I, Madalena Maria Albero, herein referred to as party of the first part, being of sane mind and good health, and acting of my own free will, hereby accept the marriage proposal offered by Antonio Vitoro Coscarelli, herein referred to as party of the second part, subject to the following stipulations:

1. *Within two weeks from signing this agreement, party of the second part will purchase a stunning, but not-too-expensive diamond ring, to be delivered to the ring-finger of party of the first part.*
2. *Party of the second part will not discuss prices, investments, or business of any kind. He will say that he pledges to love and adore party of the first part forever, as party of the first part also pledges to him.*
3. *The money saved by buying a less-expensive ring will be invested in a savings account which both parties will continue to contribute to on a monthly basis until the funds can be invested as a down-payment on a house that they both love and can afford. (See clause 4).*

4. *Party of the second part agrees to be the father of our children, (two, if possible) and both parties promise to love said children as our most valuable assets—never to treat them as possessions and never to complain about how much they cost.*

5. *Party of the second part agrees to treat our relationship as a spiritual matter that lasts forever and transcends material possessions and the worries of daily living. He will never spell out what our love is worth in monetary terms or turn our love into a business deal. This clause is non-negotiable.*

6. *If party of the second part agrees to the terms, then a wedding will be scheduled no later than one year from the signing of this agreement.*

Signed by the parties, on this _____ day of _____, 20__.

Antonio Vitori Coscarelli _____
Madalena Maria Albero _____

Madi had it right. Tony was totally turned on. He was breathing hard, his pupils dilated, his armpits sweating. It was primal; she had tapped into the wildest fantasies of the man with whom she was going to spend the rest of her life. And she felt like a sex goddess.

"So," he said slowly, "your answer is yes?"

"My answer is yes, yes, and no. Yes, I will marry you. Yes, I want the diamond ring. And no—I don't like it when you treat our relationship like a business deal. Love lasts forever; it's a *spiritual force!*"—she swept her hand across the table, really finding her rhythm—"It *transcends* the material world. You shouldn't put conditions on it. In the grand scheme of things, love is all that is real, despite what your accounting professors taught you. Without love, nothing else matters. Promise me you'll remember that."

"I'll try not to get too materialistic." But Tony didn't really understand what she was getting at.

"Look, Tony. Love isn't a little thing; it doesn't just happen. It takes over your entire life. It's forever. I need to know that our relationship isn't a business deal to you, that you're not in it when it's working and bailing when it's inconvenient. Do you understand the difference between spirituality and materialism?"

"Sure," Tony replied.

Madi stared at him for a moment before extending her hand. "Deal or no deal?"

"Deal." And they shook on it. They both signed the contract, hugged and kissed, and Madi broke into tears right there in the Coffee Bean Cafe. She squirreled the contract into her purse for safe-keeping, and they headed to her apartment where they sealed the deal behind closed doors.

Living on Parallel Planes

Tony and Madi are about to celebrate their tenth wedding anniversary and, needless to say, things have changed. For one, they have two incredible daughters, Angela and Andrea, ages seven and eight, respectively. For another,

Tony has earned the right to flex his accounting muscles. He has built a hugely successful accounting practice with a stable of clients including music stars, television personalities, and sports millionaires.

Tony and Madi are packing their Lexus for a spring break in Florida. Tony holds a clipboard with a list on it and as he goes down the list, Madi, who is squished in the back seat, checks to make sure every item is packed where it should be. List-checking is a ritual Madi has learned to tolerate, and the two of them execute the drill like clockwork. Swimsuits? Check. Beach chairs? Check. Dish detergent? Check. Shampoo? Check. Toilet paper? Uncheck. Toilet paper! Angela runs to retrieve a half-dozen rolls from the bathroom closet. The list goes on: Hammer? Check. Nails? Check. Floor wax? Check. Paint? Check. Really, it's a work trip—the new condo in Florida needs repairs before they can rent it out. The girls will spend their spring break with Uncle Danny and Aunt Arianna, playing with their cousins. Madi has lectured them about the intricacies of being on good behavior.

Tony and Madi already own five condos in Florida, and buying one more sounded like one too many to Madi—more drudgery, more headaches, more items on an already-full to-do list. Of course, Tony can't focus on anything but the financial side of it. He is convinced that condos in Florida will deliver a huge return on investment someday. During the recession, people were practically giving them away. He calculated the tax advantages, rental rates, and the rising growth of tourism in Florida. He listed out the financial pluses and minuses in two columns, and Madi capitulated, too tired to fight it any longer. Once she relented, Tony negotiated a purchase price so low that he has been the talk of the country club for weeks. People in their social circle call him "Tony Lowball," but Madi knows that the guys in the locker room just call him "Lowballs." Tony hasn't changed over the years—Madi, on the other hand, has learned that too much investing in the future can create a ton of misery in the present.

The new condo is a ten-hour drive away, and Madi desperately hopes the trip won't be too much of a strain. She hasn't actually seen the condo, but the photos look nice—three bedrooms off a large family room with an open kitchen and sprawling deck overlooking the Gulf of Mexico. The beach is only three hundred feet away. Hopefully, she will carve out some time to dig her toes in the sand and get her feet wet. Waves, sand, and palm trees: she can hardly wait to watch the sun set over the Gulf, even if she is dreading all the work they have in store.

In the pre-dawn hours of the next morning, Tony backs the Lexus out of the garage and winds down the long driveway. Madi surveys their beautiful home with its security systems, elegant lighting, and manicured lawn. Never in her wildest dreams did she ever think she would be so rich. They drive down the tree-lined boulevard past the lavish homes of their gated community and turn onto the freeway.

The car is eerily quiet as they make their way out of Lovejoy and into the mountains. They haven't gone far before Madi falls into a peaceful trance. Her senses heighten to experience the intricate details of the barns, pastures, and tree-covered hills that dot the landscape. She feels a special kinship with people who live in the small enclaves along the route, and pays attention to exit signs for towns that she normally drives past without a second glance. She is mesmerized by the sun peeking over the distant horizon, and takes note of how it casts long shadows across barely-budding trees. *What an awesome day to be alive*, she tells herself.

Suddenly, she feels an icy breeze brush across her cheeks. Before she knows what's happening, she feels as if she's alone in the car, in the country, in the whole world: what's the point of another condo? What's the point of anything? A tremor runs up Madi's spine. Instinctively, she turns to the man she loves. The silhouette of Tony's face is lit up by the warm, gentle rays of the rising sun. Madi exhales and smiles as the cold fades, and color seems to return to the landscape. She cannot touch the love she feels, but she knows it is real. She feels it inside her. Every cell of her body tingles with it. All that remains of her sudden despair is a gentle sense of peace. As the last memories of the terror slip away, Madi pledges to never let another condo, a long to-do list, or another investment put a dent in the love she feels for Tony. Not today. Not ever.

Madi reaches in her purse and pulls out the contract she and Tony signed over ten years ago. She can't help but cringe at it now. *Once an accountant, always an accountant.*

"Do you ever think that we work too hard?" she asks.

"What do you mean 'work too hard?'"

"Well, don't you think that maybe we have too much stuff? I mean, do we really need this Lexus? And isn't this new condo biting off more than we can chew?"

"You're tired. Why don't you close your eyes and get some sleep?" Tony glances down at the paper in her hand. "Oh, you're reading that contract again."

"I'm looking it over for old times' sake. You know, life is short, Tony. The girls are growing up fast. And you and I have become more like business partners than lovers. You promised that wasn't going to happen; it's right here in the contract. When are we going to cut back on investing in the future and start living?"

"Most people would die for the lifestyle we live."

"We have the lifestyle, yes. But are we living the life? I don't find the same fulfillment in possessions that you do—material things aren't all that real to me. That's all I am trying to say."

"That sounds enlightened, like something a new-age guru would peddle," Tony snickers. "Why would you say our possessions aren't real?"

"Because material possessions don't stand the test of time—they come and go. Sooner or later, this Lexus will end up in a scrap heap. These designer clothes will disintegrate. And that house we live in will be torn down and forgotten. You might think this stuff is worth building a life around, but there's a whole other universe out there—a spiritual universe you can't touch or see. It's real, though. That's the way I look at the world."

"I love this Lexus," Tony counters. "And let's hope it's real because we are doing seventy-five right now. If it isn't real, we've got a little problem." He raps his knuckles on the dash. "Sounds real to me. Manufactured right here in America—not imported from heaven." Tony's sarcasm is over the top, and he figures he better shut up. He turns on a classic rock station, and the radio blares.

All we are is dust in the wind . . .

"There's nothing wrong with being a realist," Tony shouts over the music.

"It depends on what you call real," Madi shouts back. "Someday you're going to understand that love is the only thing that is real—nothing else matters. And I'm dying to see that day."

The song is over, and so is their conversation. Madi slips the contract back into her purse. And as they barrel down the freeway, Tony does some meditation of his own.

The exterior doors are rusty. Replace or repair? Cheaper to repair but no tax deduction. Replace costs more, but it's a deduction. Solution: put Madi on the payroll to repair the doors, charge her wages to the repair budget, and get the tax deduction. Keep the money in the family. Brilliant idea. Brilliant.

What's Going On?

The next thing Tony hears is ping . . . ping . . . ping. A blinding light is trying to pry open his eyes, but he fights to keep them shut. His chest weighs a ton, his heart and lungs feel like they've set up shop next to his spine. He wants to sit up, but can't; he wants to cry out, but can't do that either. His body shivers. His head throbs mercilessly. He shifts a leg, then wiggles his toes. Everything moves— but barely. He maneuvers a hand to his face, and his suspicions are confirmed: something has gone terribly wrong. His eyes are swollen and caked with blood. Painfully, he allows one eye to open, and the eyeball slowly works its way down his chest to his belly. He is completely draped in white. *What's going on?*

Before he can panic, a warm wave of peace drifts over him. He squints his eyes and sees at last the Queen of Beauty hovering above him. Every color in the universe beams from her face and her smile wraps him in joy. Her voice is the hallelujah chorus. Watching her lips, Tony finally realizes what she is saying: "Wake up, Tony. Wake up. Wake up, Tony." Every cell in his body begins to celebrate: *What an awesome day to be alive.*

"Madi?" he breathes out.

"Of course it's me, silly. You don't think I would let you wake up all by yourself, do you?" Madi caresses his hand and touches his shoulder.

"My God, am I happy to see you. What's going on?"

"Let's just say that we ran into 'a little problem' on the freeway. And that Lexus you love is going to the scrap heap a lot sooner than you thought it would."

"Don't worry," Tony says, "insurance will take care of it; we have full replacement coverage."

Madi rolls her eyes. She wraps her arms around his trembling body and whispers in his ear, "Tony, we don't have time for nonsense like that. Big changes are coming. But I promise to cover you. We'll handle it together, as a couple, like we do with everything."

"You're scaring me," he tells her.

"Don't be afraid . . . you are going to hear a rumor. Tell yourself it isn't true. Promise you won't believe a word of what you hear."

"Like what?"

"You'll know it when you hear it. I'm not letting you fall back asleep until you promise not to believe it."

"I promise," he says, although he has no idea what she is asking of him.

"For now, lie here and rest. And remember I love you—that's forever. I have to go now, but I'll come back as soon as I can." And she disappears.

Tony fades in and out of consciousness for what could be three minutes or three hours. Eventually, he falls into a deep, deep sleep.

I Owe My Life to Lexus

"Good morning, Antonio," says the nurse, examining Tony's gauze-wrapped head. "You've been sleeping since yesterday. These bandages look good, so we'll leave them in place and give everything time to heal. Your eyes are probably sore, but whatever you do, don't touch them. Do you want something to eat?"

"I'm not hungry," says Tony.

"Do you remember how you got here?"

"Not really."

Just then, a voice bellows from across the room, "Welcome back, bro. You've been asleep for twenty-four hours."

Tony smiles. It's a voice he's known all his life, "Danny!"

"You've got some nasty cuts and bruises, bro."

"What happened?" asks Tony.

"Details later, but let's just say you didn't get far on that trip to Florida. A trucker in the lane next to you had a heart attack. Lost control. Clipped you from the side. Christie Truitt says you probably never saw it coming."

"I don't remember a thing," says Tony, reaching for his eye.

"Don't rub your eyes!" Danny barks.

"How are the girls?" asks Tony.

"They're doing as well as can be expected. Staying at our place for the time being. Don't worry; Arianna is taking care of them. Thank God they weren't in the car with you."

"I owe my life to Lexus," says Tony.

"Lexus is a safe car, bro, but Madi is the one who had your back. Truitt says Madi insisted that the paramedics take care of you and the trucker first. She waited to go last and wouldn't let them help her until you were on your way to the hospital."

"Thanks for letting me know; Madi would never tell me that."

"Yep. Madi was a real hero." Danny pauses for several seconds, then says, "You better get some rest before you start thinking about anyone else."

The nurse agrees: "Get all the sleep you can, Tony. Those cuts and bruises need to heal." She smiles and points her finger at Danny. "You—go take a shower. You look like you just finished a mud run."

Danny winks at the nurse. "Maria has ordered me to take a shower, bro. I've been wearing the same clothes for two days. Rumor has it I'm stinking up the place."

"I don't believe in rumors," Tony mumbles, wondering whether this is what Madi meant. Then he giggles, euphoric just to be alive.

"I wish it was only a rumor," Maria teases, holding her nose as she motions Danny out the door.

Hospitals are Hotbeds of Rumor

Tony lies there for a minute. "Speaking of rumors, Maria, have you heard anything about my wife?"

"I heard she saved your life. It was in the news this morning. Everyone is talking about it. Other than that, I wouldn't believe half of what I hear around here. Hospitals are hotbeds of rumors and misinformation."

"Do you know where Madi is?"

"Madi? Who is Madi?" Maria seems stupefied.

"Madi, my wife."

"Oh, you mean Madalena. Wow, I didn't realize you call her Madi. That's a sweet name." Maria bends over, lowers her voice, and says, "You know she's no longer in the hospital, right?"

"Yes, I do know. She was here yesterday and we talked. She had to leave for a little while. I thought maybe you saw her come back while I was asleep."

Maria thinks for a moment. "No, I didn't see her, but

I'll ask around." She pops out the door and disappears down the hallway.

I've Got It Covered

No sooner is Maria gone when Madi shows up again. "Sweet, sweet, sweet," she says mimicking the nurse. "I've been called 'sweet' all my life."

"You are sweet," Tony tells her.

"Well, the days of sweet are over!"

"Hey, there's no reason to cop an attitude: I told you insurance is going to take care of everything. I've got it covered."

"And I told you—we don't have time for nonsense." Then Madi snuggles up to Tony's sore body, and whispers, "Did you hear the rumor?"

"I heard you're a hero."

"That's ridiculous! Anyone would have done what I did. You were teetering on the edge of life; the truck driver was near death. I didn't have a scratch on me. So I told the paramedics to take you in one ambulance and the truck driver in the other. I waited for the third. It made total sense."

"I owe my life to you and Lexus. When things get back to normal—"

"—We are never going back to normal, Tony. You have to get ready for what's coming."

"You are really scaring me."

"There are reasons to be scared. Trust our love; it's forever. We have to stick together."

Voices echo down the hallway and Madi hurriedly says, "I have to go. I'm heading to Arianna's to check on Andrea and Angela. I'll come back as soon as possible. Be strong, and remember what you promised. Don't believe a word these people say. And tell them to quit calling me Madalena—my name is Madi!" She slips into the hallway and scurries away from the voices.

Mousey Guy

"Hey, bro," Danny calls out as he walks through the door. A guy with mousey brown hair marches in unison behind him, and Maria keeps step in third place. Judging by their gait, Tony judges they're on some kind of mission. He takes one look at mousey guy and somehow recognizes the shape of his teeth, the lines on his face, the curve of his nose. Tony has seen this face before. Mousey guy doesn't introduce himself, but walks over and tugs on Tony's bandages. "Nice work, even if I do say so myself."

Maria clears her throat. "Doctor Murphy has information for you on the whereabouts of your wife."

Danny, frowning, scoots across the room and stares out the window. Doctor Murphy pulls up a chair, settles himself, and clears his throat before he opens his mouth. "Ahem. I am Dr. Brendan Murphy, the physician who treated you and Madalena after the accident. I'm glad we are finally getting a chance to talk."

"Madi," interjects Tony.

"Madi?" asks the doctor.

"Madi. Her name is Madi."

"Oh, I get it. You call her Madi. What a sweet name," says the doctor.

Sweet, sweet, sweet clangs through Tony's head, but he keeps his mouth shut.

"I'm sorry, but by the time Madi got to the emergency room, the pulmonary contusion was massive."

"Pulmonary contusion?"

"Trauma to the lungs and heart. It happens occasionally—someone feels perfectly fine after a crash and then collapses later due to bleeding around the heart and lungs. On a scale of one to ten, the internal damage was eight or nine. I am sorry to say that we lost her."

"Lost? She's not lost. She was here a few minutes ago. She went to check on our daughters, but I'm expecting her back in a little while."

The room goes silent. Danny turns toward him. "We lost Madi, bro. I should have told you sooner."

A cold breeze smacks Tony in the face, but he blows it off. "No, no, no. I know Madi. She might be a little shaken up by the accident, but she wouldn't disappear. She went to check on Andrea and Angela—she'll be back soon. Danny, call Arianna and find out for yourself."

"Your wife is not coming back. She succumbed to her injuries in the emergency room at eleven-forty-four yesterday," Dr. Murphy pronounces, with all the authority that a physician can carry.

Tony squeezes his puffy eyes shut. But when he opens them, Dr. Brendan Murphy is still sitting in the chair. Danny is back by the window, and Maria is looking on with her mouth wide open.

At that moment, a gale slams Tony with hurricane force, flips him topsy-turvy, and drops him on a frozen Cliffside.

Turning away from the abyss, he glances once more over the shoulder of Dr. Murphy and sees Madi in the hallway. And what does she do? She spells *R-U-M-O-R* with her fingers. She shakes her head, *Do not believe it!* She loops her finger around her head, *The doctor is looney tunes.*

Tony remembers Madi's words: *Trust our love; it's forever. We have to stick together.* With Madi cheering from the hallway, Tony slams his eyes shut. He turns on Dr. Murphy: "You may have graduated from medical school, Doc, but what makes you an authority on life and death?"

"I know this is hard for you, but your wife is deceased. It's a medical fact, and you have to accept it."

"I appreciate everything you did for me in the ER, Doc, but you better check out your medical facts because you're wrong. Madi is not dead. I've been talking to her, and she is standing outside the door right now. So stop spreading rumors about my wife."

Tony turns to his big brother. "Danny, go out in the hallway and tell Madi to come in here!"

Danny stands and shrugs his shoulders.

Dr. Murphy snorts. "I was hoping to discharge you tomorrow morning—you will be well enough physically, but I can't let you leave the hospital with these paranoid delusions. You need to accept reality. Your wife is dead."

The doctor rises to his feet, hands above his head as if to say, "I tried," and backs toward the door, all the while barking orders to Maria.

As the nurse and doctor head out the door, Tony shouts, "What do you know? You don't even know her name. Her name is Madi. Don't call her Madalena again."

Pull it Together, Bro

Danny can't take his eyes off Tony. "Have you lost your mind?" He sits in the chair, and the two brothers stare at one another like two men on opposite sides of a road, wondering which way the other will go. Minutes go by.

Finally, Danny breaks the silence. "You're in shock, Tony."

"I'm shocked you would play with my head like this. It's misguided. And mean. And I'm not falling for it."

"You heard the doctor. Madi is gone. She's not in the hallway. She isn't coming back."

"You have to believe me, Danny. I've seen her. I've talked with her. I'm surprised you would fall for medical quackery like this."

"Whoa, you have to pull it together, bro. You're supposed to be discharged tomorrow. Angela and Andrea need you to be strong. That doctor isn't going to let you go home until you face reality."

"It depends on what you call real," Tony mutters.

Silence takes over again, and the two men sit and fidget. Finally, Tony says, "Get lost. I need to talk to Madi."

"Will you be okay here by yourself?"

"I'm not by myself! I told you I am going to talk to Madi!"

"Okay," says Danny, hands in the air. "I'm going to the chapel. And when I come back, we're going to talk about this some more. This is all my fault. I should have told you sooner."

"Just go!"

You've Got Some Explaining to Do

With Danny out of the way, Tony calls out for Madi. The room lights up again. "Way to go," she cheers. "For a minute there, I thought you were going to fall for that medical garbage. Good for you! You fought off the doom and gloom."

"You've got some explaining to do."

"About what?"

"About what? About the doctor. That's what. Why would he say you are gone?"

"That's easy to explain. He's a doctor. To him, I am gone. But what does he know? He doesn't even know my name. How could he understand the bond that holds you and me together? Love is forever. Remember, Tony? You are going to love me forever, aren't you? Because right now, I feel more alive than ever."

"You feel alive. Well, isn't that amazing," he says. "What I want to know is: are you really alive?"

"That depends on what you call real," Madi argues.

"How am I supposed to love you if you aren't real?"

Madi's smile sours. "Oh, I get it. Is being alive another one of your conditions all of a sudden? My God, I love you, laugh with you, cry over you, sleep with you, birth your girls, and I've been doing it for over ten years. Every minute of every day, I have been alive for you. And all of a sudden, when I'm not parading around the house at your beck and call, it's *hasta la vista,* baby? I should have listened to my girlfriends a long time ago. Is me being here to work your daily grind all our love means to you?"

"Excuse me, I had no idea you were being so literal about this forever thing."

"Don't get snarky with me. You're running out of time. You signed the contract. We sealed the deal. Are you going to hold up your end of the bargain or not? I'm not asking you to stop counting things, Tony—I'm asking you to start counting things that really matter." On that note, Madi storms out the door.

Tony holds his throbbing head in his hands, and watches the room swirl in circles around him.

Bring in the Priest

No sooner is Madi gone, when Danny bursts through the door. This time big brother isn't bringing in a doctor; he's bringing in a priest. Miles is wearing his white collar under a black leather Harley jacket and his biker boots thud, thud, thud as he walks in. A pair of cheap sunglasses accent his well-seasoned face. The man in black slips off his oversized gloves and pries a gorgeous brunette off of his arm.

Danny sets the wheels in motion: "Tony, Father Miles wants to talk to you. You know Alexa, right? Alexa, star witness in the driving while texting case? Maria's little sister, Alexa? Charlie's Alexa?"

"Oh, that Alexa." Tony purses his lips. "Hmm."

Miles smiles. "I hope you don't mind Alexa being here. I'm her spiritual advisor. We're going out on the town this evening, and I asked her to join me for this. She's dying to see a man of God in action."

In true form, Danny slides across the room to stare out the window. Surprisingly, Alexa glides over and stands almost inappropriately close to him.

"Just call me Miles. I'm too young to be your father," says the clergyman, winking in the direction of Alexa. He sits down with Tony. "Tony, it seems that life has done what life does best—thrown you a curve ball. Maybe I can help."

Tony blurts out everything. "Miles, my wife and I were in a car wreck. I don't remember what happened. Everyone is telling me Madi is gone. But she has been here talking to me. So I don't know whether she is here or whether she is gone. I don't know what to think. On top of that, some freaky force is dogging me. It's like a cold wind—an empty, dreadful feeling—like a specter that wants to drag me into a black hole."

"The Cold Wind of Despair?"

"I've never heard of that, but it sounds about right. It feels like something sinister."

"Tony, don't get tangled up with the Cold Wind of Despair; it's evil," warns the priest. "Let me ask a couple of questions. When you talk to Madi, does she appear as a beam of light?"

"Absolutely. With every color in the universe."

"And does she have a message for you? A message for your own good?"

"Those are her exact words," Tony swears. "So you believe me when I say that she talks to me?"

"Of course I believe you. Why wouldn't she talk to you? It's only common sense."

"Nobody else around here believes it. They keep telling me Madi is dead, but I know she isn't."

Miles squints, purses his lips, leans in, and on the hush-hush says, "You and Madi are communicating in ways that medical science doesn't understand. Madi sounds like an angel to me. She could be on a mercy mission."

"Whoa, Miles, don't go off half-cocked. I didn't say anything about harps or halos. I'm an accountant; I stick to reality."

"It depends on what you call real. Angels are real. They have been visiting us since the dawn of time. They bring us knowledge from the spiritual world, information about things that we can't see. Everyone needs an angel in their life."

"She isn't behaving like an angel. She worked herself into quite a temper today."

"Don't be so hard on her. She needs time to learn. It's only been two days, hasn't it? In my humble opinion, she is behaving like a perfect angel—she is trying to bring you a message. I suggest you listen to her, my friend, and do what she tells you to do."

"You talk like you know her," says Tony.

"Well, I understand her. I talked with Madi in the

emergency room after the accident. We shared a moment together."

Tony feels tears flood his eyes. He blinks them away and clutches Miles' outstretched hand. "So Madi talks to you, too?" he whispers.

"Wait a minute. I said I *talked* with her. Past tense. I was holding her hand when she left this world."

Tony pulls him closer. "Tell me, Miles. What did she say?"

"Madi said quite a bit about you and your daughters. In fact, you were all she talked about. In my experience, at the end, everyone thinks about people they love. They never talk about jobs, homes, cars, clothes, money; nothing you can see or touch. In the end, the invisible is all that's real. Love is the final thing. Without it, nothing matters."

"You sound just like Madi."

"Tony, there is something you need to know. Madi wasn't afraid to die. She was at peace with herself. But she didn't feel that same peace for you. She was troubled about leaving you; you were unfinished business to her. If I had to guess, I would say she is hanging around to tie up loose ends with you. She wants to set you on a path before she leaves this planet. Angels can't stay here forever, you know. You may be holding her back from where she has to go."

"I'm no good for Madi," Tony laments. "She wants me to say I will love her forever. I've searched my heart, but I don't find eternal love there. I don't know if I believe in eternity."

"You're looking in the wrong place. You don't find

spiritual love in your heart. You find it in those around you. It's a gift. Receive it, Tony. And once you allow eternal love to surround you, you will be able to treasure Madi, and care for her properly. I'm going to pray that you will be enlightened about this."

"No offense, Father, but I need more than a prayer right now. This is a stretch for me. I'm an accountant; I count what's real. If I can't see it or touch it, I don't relate to it. I'm not on board when it comes to spiritual matters."

Miles slaps his knee, abruptly stands up, and shoves his palm at Tony. "I'm warning you! Stop tormenting that woman. The only thing standing between you and the Cold Wind of Despair is the love Madi gives you. Thank God, she doesn't pussy-foot around like you. If she were my daughter, I'd tell her to get off this planet now and let the Cold Wind of Despair swallow you whole. Is that what you want, Tony? To be eaten alive by hatred, indifference, and desolation?"

Tony winces. He has never dealt with an angry priest before.

"I didn't think so," Miles pronounces. "So here's my blessing: Quit whining and give Madi what she deserves— for your own good. Trust her. Let her guide you. Quit looking in your selfish heart, and open your eyes to the spiritual universe. That's where you will find the love you're looking for. And when you find it, you will cherish Madi. You will adore her. You will never stop loving her. Now, she can't hang around this planet forever. So do it— and I don't want to hear another word out of you."

Tony and Danny stare in utter shock. Miles turns to Alexa and gives her a warm smile. "You see, my dear, God doesn't coddle weakness. Sometimes a priest has to roll heads to get the Lord's work done. Tony is lucky to have a woman like Madi—she's a saint. He doesn't deserve her, but if he knows what's good for him, he is going to grow a pair and quit playing games with her."

Bittersweet

Miles takes Alexa's arm. "We'd best get back," he says, glancing at Tony. "Goodbye—and remember, listen to your wife."

Danny turns. "Let me show you to the elevator."

Alexa struts down the hall, still hanging on Miles' arm, and Danny trails her like a lost puppy, panting to get close. But when the elevator door closes on the soon-to-be revelers, Danny breathes a bittersweet sigh of relief.

She's gone.

On his walk back, Danny comes upon a business card laying in the hallway. He picks it up and his fingers clench down hard. *Alexa Arioli, Assistant to the Chief Executive Officer, Macklin Media*—complete with all her contact information. Immediately, his body shifts.

Oh my God. Alexa dropped this for me. She wants me to contact her.

He feels his blood pulsing in his head, his neck, everywhere.

What a coy devil, that woman. I'd nail her. Bad—really bad.

Danny whips out his wallet to bury the card inside. But

when he opens the wallet, a well-worn photo of Arianna smiles back at him. *Ugh! Not good.*

So he goes to plan B: he takes out his phone to enter Alexa's contact info. But when he opens the phone, Arianna is smiling at him from the wallpaper of his home screen. *Yikes!*

Danny's thoughts quickly wander to the Southern Region Women's Correctional Facility, the not-so-cozy place that Clare currently calls home. *All the people Clare hurt with her lies. Senseless. Stupid.*

He remembers, too, the afternoon Johanna visited his office, devastated by Brendan's dark secret, heartbroken over his carelessness. To this day, he resents Brendan for the misery he caused Arianna, who was forced to reveal his secret to Johanna. *Brendan Murphy might be a good doctor, but he is a jackass in his personal life. Unnecessary.*

And what about Liliana? All the pain Charlie caused her, playing games with Alexa. *He's my flesh and blood, but I don't want to be like him.*

Danny stands frozen, his phone is in one hand, and Alexa's business card in the other. He looks up and down the hall, not a soul in sight.

There is a trash can ten steps away. He takes a step towards it, and his leg locks and stalls. He tries another step, but feels paralyzed.

Down the hall, my little brother is fighting to hang onto the woman he loves, and here I am, playing middle-school games with Alexa.

Danny takes a deep breath. He crumples the card and

tosses it in the trash-can. With that, he heads to the hospital cafeteria for a late evening snack.

The Pinch of Time

In his room, Tony lies silent and alone, feeling the weight of what he has to do. He opens his heart, prays for strength, and calls for Madi. "I'm here," she whispers from the corner. She is fading. Gone are the brilliant colors, and her voice has lost the strong, unbridled confidence of before.

"I never dreamed it would come to this, Madi," Tony says. "You've been waiting on me for a long time. Now I have to check off a box on my to-do list. And I don't know if I can do it: I've never told you good-bye before. Not like this."

Madi moves across the room and lies down next to him. "I tried to tell you good-bye after that botched marriage proposal. My friends thought I'd leave you for sure, but I knew I would never say good-bye to you. Never. I couldn't say it then, and I still can't."

"I have a confession to make. You gave me the life of my dreams—two beautiful daughters and years of love that I didn't deserve. You carried me even when I stepped on you. I was always working to get to a better place—but you were always right where you wanted to be. I wanted stuff, but little did I know that I already had everything that matters. That was quite a contract you put together, Madi. But I got the better deal out of it."

Madi smiles. "You expressed your love in the way you

knew how, and I didn't always appreciate your hard work. I have to say good-bye now, Tony. I hoped to hang around for another thirty or forty years, but I'm out of time. Tony, is there something you want to tell me? Because I can't go in peace until you do."

"It doesn't seem fair. If I say I love you forever, I lose you for good."

"Tony, as usual, you've got it backwards. If you love me forever, you will never lose me."

Tony feels the Cold Wind of Despair blowing around his shoulders, its tendrils whispering around his ears. He turns to Madi and pushes the words out syllable by syllable. "Madalena. I will love you forever. I'm still learning what forever means, and I'm not even sure it exists, but when I get there, I will look for you. I promise."

"You'll get there, Antonio; I know you will. And when you do, I'll be waiting for you. You can count on it."

Madi vanishes, and Tony knows this time she is gone forever. For the first time since he was a little boy, Tony sobs. Every cell in his body cries out.

Setting the Record Straight

Danny returns from the cafeteria just as Maria closes Tony's door. "Go have another piece of cake. Your brother needs to be alone."

"How do you know I was eating cake?" Danny shoots back.

Maria grins. "There are crumbs all over your face. And look at your shirt. Do you need to take another shower?"

Danny wipes his shirt and clears his throat. "Tony is

going to be all right, isn't he? I can't imagine what it's like to lose someone you love."

Maria's smile wavers and falls. She turns away. "I don't have to imagine; I know. I kicked my husband to the curb. He loved me, and, looking back, I realize I loved him. But at the time, I didn't care. I got the urge to run off and do mud runs, thinking I was going to be a hot shot. I quit a good job, and worst of all, I hurt my little boy. And what do I have to show for it? A medal and a tee shirt."

"I go through periods when I get the urge to run away myself."

"You know, I met your wife at my birthday party last year. Arianna's her name?"

"Yep. Fourteen years together, her and me. Us. It can get boring you know."

"I scope people out pretty quick. She's a classy woman."

"Most people say that so you must be right."

"Can I give you a little advice? I saw you with Alexa. Be careful with my sister. Don't be like Charlie. I love Alexa, everyone does. She has a way about her—just don't lose your head over it."

Danny's face turns red and he avoids Maria's eyes.

She smiles. "Good news. Your brother is doing better; he's going to be discharged tomorrow morning. Now forget what I said about the cake; go be with him. I think he would want you there."

Maria sits down to update Tony's medical record. First, she writes the only diagnosis that Dr. Murphy will accept: *intensive care delirium has abated. No further signs of paranoia. Cleared for discharge.* Then she adds a note of her own: *patient is trying to face reality—just like the rest of us.*

Remember This Day

Early the next morning, Tony wakes up to find Danny sleeping in the chair next to him. Though his cuts and bruises will take a while to heal, Tony is ready to go home to Andrea and Angela.

Maria has packed Tony's belongings in a bag, which she hands to Danny, who stands still rubbing his tired eyes. "I have Madi's purse. Can you handle carrying a woman's purse, Mr. Big-Shot Lawyer?"

Danny chuckles, and within minutes, the two brothers are taking the long walk down to the elevator.

As Danny drives them home, Tony feels like he is on a different freeway than the one he drove a mere three days ago. All is quiet; there isn't much to say. Tony feels as if somehow he is outside of himself. He sees things he didn't used to see: the rolling mountains, the sunny colors breaking over the hills, the azure and sylvan valleys. He takes note of the names of the towns they pass, and he wonders what the people in those places are planning for today. It's just another day for them, indistinguishable from yesterday or tomorrow. But Tony will always remember this day.

Suddenly Tony realizes that he will never talk with Madi again. They will never make love, never laugh together, drink a cup, or eat a simple meal. Will he be able to give Andrea and Angela the kind of love they deserve? Through the open window, the Cold Wind of Despair seeps into the car, the cold forcing itself down his throat.

Tony grabs Madi's purse from the back seat and pulls out the contract he and Madi signed over ten years ago. He smells the fresh brews of the Coffee Bean Café. He sees the smile on Madi's face exactly as it was when she first pushed the contract across the table. He feels the texture of the satin blouse and dark suit she wore. It's as real to him now as it was then. Now, Tony understands what the signatures on that paper really mean. *Love is forever* cries out to him.

Tony feels warm again, inside and out. He breathes freely and feels safe. Right then and there, Tony vows that he is not going to let a car accident, however monumental or tragic, come between him and the woman he loves. Not now. Not ever. And that thought makes every cell in his body dance with joy. He slips the contract back into Madi's purse.

"Like my threads, bro?" Danny says at last, glancing at Tony. "Dolce & Gabbana, made in Italy. Mom always said, only the best for her boys, right?"

"That sweater is going to end up in a rag bin someday."

"You're calling a two hundred and fifty dollar sweater a rag?"

After a while, Danny speaks up again: "I'll take my BMW over your Lexus anytime."

"Your BMW is going to end up in the same place as my Lexus—the junkyard."

Danny doesn't know what to say. He opens his mouth

and shuts it again. Out of the corner of his eye, he catches Tony staring at him. "Everything okay bro?"

Tony nods slowly. "Want a condo in Florida? I'll give it to you. How's that for a deal?"

"You're not serious."

"I am serious. I don't need another condo. I'll sign it over to you, but with a warning: condos are a lot of work."

"You're still in shock, bro."

"My mind is clearer than ever," murmurs Tony.

As they drive through the tree-lined streets and manicured lawns of Tony's neighborhood, Tony pictures the mothers, fathers, and children living in these grand shells—he hopes they appreciate the love they share.

"There are some nice homes in this neighborhood," observes Danny.

"These houses will be torn down in fifty years, and the only thing these families will have left are memories—mostly good ones, if they take care of what matters."

Danny pulls up the driveway and parks. Tony climbs out and turns to his brother: "Thanks for everything, Danny. I'll see you later."

Inside, the silence is eerie. Tony goes to the master bedroom that he has shared with Madi all these years. Her pajamas lie on the bed. Her makeup is spread across the vanity, just the way she left it three days ago. Tony looks behind the bedroom door. Nothing. He goes inside the walk-in closet. Nothing in there but rows of designer clothes that will never make a sound.

He walks down the hall and checks out the girls'

bedrooms. Trophies, stuffed animals, plush bedding, expensive toys. And absolute silence.

Tony makes his way to the kitchen where morning sunlight is streaming through the window above the sink. Sunbeams swirl and animate the room.

"Let's get busy," Madi's voice says. "Andrea and Angela will be home soon, and you've got a memorial service to get ready for. Don't worry, I'll give you the words to say. No gloom and doom, please. When the girls get here, the first thing you tell them is that you will love them forever. Think you can handle that?"

Tony can't exactly see Madi—he can't touch her—but he knows she is real. And he is well aware that she loves him in ways that he is only just beginning to understand. Madi knows Tony's flaws and limitations—she knows everything about him—and she loves him anyway. He will count on that forever.

A EULOGY IN PRAISE OF FOREVER

Dear Family and Friends, we are gathered here today, in a common bond, to remember someone none of us will ever forget: the love of my life, Madalena Coscarelli. They call this a eulogy, but keep in mind that Madi is here with us. I look at our amazing daughters sitting in the front row, and watch Angela push her hair to the side in exactly the same way her mother did. In Andrea, I see the twinkle of her mother's eyes. Madi lives on in you and me, and in all those she touched in her too-short life. The words you hear from my mouth come from Madi. Those of you who know me know I could never get up and speak with any eloquence at all without Madi to prop me up. Everyone needs an angel in their life. I have mine with me today, and I hope you have yours.

When I was in college, I was required to read a book by an ancient philosopher named Plato, from whom comes the idea of "platonic love." Plato had a strange idea that the world we live in is not real; it's temporary, crumbles easily, and has no lasting value. He believed that we are surrounded by a spiritual world of which we see only glimpses that is more real than this world in which we live, is eternal, stable, and inherently valuable. At the time, I thought this whole idea was asinine, and wasted no time telling the professor that this guy Plato was nuts.

Then along came Madi. As Father Miles can attest, Madi was not an avid church-goer, but she was intensely spiritual. Madi had a faith that was deep and genuine; she understood things about life and love that most of us don't. She lived with one foot firmly planted in Lovejoy, and the other in a universe that was bigger than her. She wasn't a dreamer; she was practical in day-to-day activities, but she always kept the grander scheme of the universe in the back of her mind. This past week, Madi has inspired me to think about the meaning of love, and I thank Father Miles for encouraging me to share my thoughts with you today.

We live in Lovejoy. It's a happy place, but we are awfully busy. There are deadlines to meet, mouths to feed, and bills to be paid. We are quite accustomed to budgets, calendars, to-do lists, clocks, making up reasons for why we do what we do, and making excuses for why we don't do what we should. For example, if you're like most people, you probably weigh a little more than you'd like, and one of these days you're going to do something about it. But not this week; you don't have time to think about it right now. I would bet there are several changes you'd like to make to improve your life, if only you had more time. Of course, you've been saying that for a long time now. In Lovejoy, we are trapped by the forces of gravity and time.

Madi's life has not turned out the way she planned; neither has mine, and you may say the same. We can't see the future. We don't know everything that will come to pass. Today we come together to face the somber fact that the best-laid plans can fall apart in the turn of a news cycle. Gravity and time turned ugly on the freeway last Tuesday and my Madi became a textbook case of being in the wrong place at the wrong time. The police report calls it an accident, even though everything that happened on the freeway last Tuesday followed the precise laws of gravity and time. Father Miles might say that there are no accidents; the Creator is in charge and has a plan even when we don't understand it or get to vote on it. Accident or not, it hurts to lose a loving mother, caring wife, loyal friend, devoted daughter, life-long sister, aunt, and cousin. My heart aches, and your presence here suggests you feel the pain as well.

In Lovejoy, gravity and time flow through us and around us, but they don't belong to us. We didn't create them. We don't own them. Nobody put us in charge of them. We're merely along for the ride. We carry our own baggage and move quickly—we're just passing through.

If you live in Lovejoy, I bet your commute to work takes roughly an hour out of your day—a half-hour to get there and another half-hour back home. That's on a good day. But have you ever stopped to think that a mere hundred miles from here—a hundred miles straight up and out into space—you could easily fly across North America in twenty minutes? You see, there's nothing to slow you down or get in the way out there. Out there, gravity is small and time is big. For all we know, time goes on forever out there.

Out in the galaxy, love is unadulterated and pure; but here in Lovejoy, love is, shall we say earthy? It's mixed with sweat, spit, blood, tears, semen, hormones gone mad, and bodily fluids we can't even identify—maybe some that don't even have a name.

When you're out in space, love will always find you. Love will fly over every hurdle, and open every locked door. In our little city, love may have to wait—we're stuck in traffic, hijacked by mom-duties, stuck paying bills, recovering from surgery, or sidelined with injuries.

In The Milky Way, everyone looks like a movie star, stays young forever, and gets the love they want—even if they have to wait for the happy ending. In Lovejoy, we get the flu, post-partum blues, eating disorders, erectile dysfunction, low-testosterone, stretch marks, and urinary tract infections. Sometimes, it's just a bad hair day.

In the spiritual world, money has nothing to do with love. But here in Lovejoy, we really do want the ring, the Lexus, the house with the pool and two-car garage. Make that a three-car garage if you get the big bonus. A beachside condo isn't a bad idea either. In Lovejoy, money can't buy love, but it can buy a darn good imitation.

Out of respect for Madi, I'm not going to lie. Madi and I shared the same address, but we lived in parallel worlds.

We were heading in the same direction, but taking different modes of transportation. Madi was flying in the spiritual universe; living grand and lofty in a world that goes on forever. I, on the other hand, was driving the congested surface-route, bogged down in bumper-to-bumper traffic and, I'm ashamed to admit, keeping one eye on the exit at all times. I played the game of love with a calculator, keeping track of costs and benefits, and too often asking Madi, "What have you done for me lately?" When loving got tough, I made the mistake of thinking that love was not working. When love became work, I treated Madi as a business partner, while Madi always viewed me as her soul mate, her one-and-only. What's the difference? Business partners can be replaced; soul mates are forever. In the day to day grind of life, maybe none of this matters, but I am sure I made Madi's life, and mine, more difficult than it needed to be.

Before you think I have totally lost my mind, let me assure you that I understand we live in a push-and-shove world, pinned down and under siege by gravity and time. In the blink of an eye, life can turn into a battlefield of dog-eat-dog, double-crossing, corporate take-overs, and economic upheaval. I don't know about you, but I feel terrified when I think I might be losing the battle. I compensated for this by hiding my fears. On the outside, I exude confidence. I appear cool, prepared, and precise, but that exterior never fooled Madi. And I hope it doesn't fool you, either.

Despite my smug grin and snarky attitude, I am more

often than not jelly on the inside. I hid my fears by piling up possessions, amassing wealth, and playing games with condos and a fancy Lexus. Last Tuesday, I was barreling down the freeway, arrogantly thinking I had everything under control, when in fact I was utterly unprepared for the cold, chaotic forces that my daughters and I have been fighting this past week. Trust me: Death—the emperor of all endings—doesn't blink an eye in the face of wealth, prestige, and power. My great sadness is that I am suffering the worst of all endings—I am losing a love that I never completely claimed or fulfilled in the first place. I let gravity hold me back, took Madi for granted, and ran out of time. Still, despite my many mistakes and shortcomings, Madi took me on a journey above and beyond to where no couple has gone before.

Don't get me wrong. I love Madi. I was totally faithful and devoted to her. But in the last few days, I have been asking myself questions that I should have asked a long time ago. Did I express my love to Madi in ways that mattered to her? Or did I love her in my own fashion, in ways that felt good to me? Did I really listen to her needs and desires? Or did I pretend to hear, then dismiss her and put my needs ahead of hers? Did I spend enough time thinking about what life was like for her? If I have learned anything in the past week, it's that feeling love for Madi wasn't enough; I needed to think a little more about how I expressed my love.

What we do with gravity and time says a lot about who we are and how we will be remembered. I look among you and can tell what you will be remembered for and why. Miles Joyce is a priest who will be remembered for his prayers and blessings. Christie Truitt asks questions; she believes in truth and justice. Dr. McDowell loves his patients and medicine; he will be remembered as a healer. Alexa Arioli will be remembered for her way of turning life in her direction. My brother Danny has always liked to argue, and he turns out to be a lawyer. My passion in life is for numbers; to a fault, really, and that's why I'm an accountant. What you do with gravity and time, makes you, *you*. What I do, makes me, *me*.

Madi lived on the border between simple little Lovejoy and the never-ending spiritual universe. She navigated both worlds. When time and gravity came for her, she wasn't afraid to walk across the border. She will be remembered as a hero for what she did on the freeway last Tuesday. She freely and voluntarily gave her life. All I can add to her remembrance is this: Madi, if giving your life for someone makes you a hero, you have been my hero for over ten years, and you will be forever.

THE HAPPY ENDING

Now, dear reader, you've finished your visit to Lovejoy. I'm sure you're tired; we can be a lot of work. You combed through our minds, felt our joy, laughed with us, cried with us, and rooted for us in our darkest hours. You had dinner in our restaurants, sat in our coffee shops, eavesdropped in our bedrooms. You hung out in a tattoo parlor, did a mud run, and visited someone in prison. You even met an angel. I hope you felt proud to be among us, even for a short while. Forgive us if we made your visit more difficult than it needed to be. We don't always live up to our own hopes and expectations. We know we could do better, if only we weren't so human.

This book never was about us, though—it's about you. What matters is what you learned about yourself. I hope you did your self-reflection, and from that perhaps you got a new perspective on yourself and someone you love. If you are determined to be more careful and thoughtful in the future, then I can only believe that you got what you came looking for. Surely, by now you've come to some conclusions about what love means to you. If so, I've done my job, and will take my leave.

Before I go, however, I have to make a confession of my own. I began writing *Cupid on Trial* thinking that I would be able to define love. That was foolish on my part, and I learned a valuable lesson: I don't believe we can define love—it's too vast and complicated to squeeze into my little book. It spans the universe, fuels our future, and is woven into the fabric of our daily lives. While we can't define love, I do believe that love defines us—if we let it. What I mean is that every chance we get to choose love is an opportunity to declare who we are and what we stand for. I try to think about that every day, and I hope you will too.

I leave you with the blessing of Father Miles Joyce: May your hearts be pure and your intentions inspired. May your minds be open and your actions kind. May you remember that what you do today, and every day, defines your life. And may you never forget: love is forever.

DISCUSSION QUESTIONS

PREFACE

1. Can you think of a time when the love someone had for you picked you up, set you on course, or kept you from going over the edge?

2. Has the love you feel for someone ever changed who you are—molded your character, made you a better person?

3. How is contemporary love, romance, and sexuality different from your parents' generation?

4. Has your dark side—your human shortcomings or limitations—ever wrecked a relationship or harmed someone you love?

5. How do you know that you love yourself? What evidence is there?

6. Tell yourself a story about someone's relationship, real or imaginary, that has affected you.

WELCOME TO LOVEJOY

7. Suppose something strange happened tonight, and you woke up tomorrow to discover that you've been mysteriously transformed into your partner. Thinking carefully about how you treat him or her, would you like to trade places?

BE STRONG

8. Have you ever experienced a flashback? What was it like? How did you feel?

9. How do you feel about the way Liliana was pushed around by Charlie?

10. Cancer changes everything, yes, but so do other conditions and events. Have you ever had a condition or been in a situation that changed everything?

11. Think about a situation where your self-image changed quickly and dramatically, like Lily. Where it changed for the worst. For the better. How quick was it? How pervasive was the change?

12. Liliana feels magnetically attracted to Aiden and Aoife Murphy. The story never says why, but most people have a theory. What is your theory?

13. As a general rule, people believe that it takes a long time to change, when sometimes all you have to do is make up your mind that you want to change. Do you believe people can change rather quickly or not?

14. How do you feel about Lily's father, Clark Macklin?

15. Why do you think that Lily went into Dante and Pauli's bedroom before she woke Charlie up on that fateful night?

16. Why would Lily keep Alexa at Macklin Media as her personal assistant? Would that be difficult? Awkward? Wrong? Or was it a perfect move on Lily's part? Would you have the strength to accept Alexa and lay the blame completely on Charlie? Or is Lily completely wrong in not putting some of the blame on Alexa?

A JOURNAL I ONCE KEPT

17. One of my favorite authors, Isak Dinesen (Out of Africa) wrote: "God made the world round so we would never be able to see too far down the road." How does that apply to Lily as she begins her Taste of Italy journal? Has this idea ever applied to you?

18. Lily says, "He's a rock, and I'm a flower." What does that mean to you?

19. What would cause Charlie to think he could get involved with Alexa and get away with it? What was he thinking?

20. Lily faces the fact that her family doesn't know how to communicate about difficult issues. Many families would say the same. How do you explain that?

21. Lily feels demeaned that Charlie doesn't tell her he plans to play golf in Cinque Terre. How does a couple decide what to share with one another? When does a secret become a lie?

22. Lily refers to "locker room talk" among the girls at work. Do women have locker room talk and how does it compare to the locker room talk of men?

PRETTY IN WHITE

23. So much of love and romance is put into boxes labeled man-woman or male-female. Can you imagine the experience of not fitting neatly into the assumed male or female identity?

24. How does your gender identity impact who you have loved or hope you will love?

25. Johanna maintains her dignity by realizing that the craziness isn't in her, it's in the expectations people have of her. What does that mean to you?

26. Johanna is what psychologists call "resilient." Google resilience and try to wrap your head around whether "resilient" applies to you.

27. Some people would call Johanna "intersexed," though I can tell you she would never apply that term to herself. How much did you know about Disorders of Sexual Development before reading her story? What have you learned from the story?

28. According to Johanna, it's not helpful to dwell on the past. Yet so many people do. Do you know anyone who spends too much energy nursing past hurts and injustices? Can you see how dwelling on the past can cause a person to waste his or her life?

29. Brendan "conveniently forgot" to reveal his secret to Johanna, thinking it was in *her* best interest. I call these self-serving beliefs, and we all have them. Are you working off of self-serving beliefs and if so, why?

30. Johanna was fortunate to be born to admirably caring parents. We can't choose our biological parents, but if we could, would you choose your parents? Before you answer that, ask yourself if your children would choose you if they could.

31. Mr. McFadden, Johanna's father, says, "I didn't know I wanted a baby with CAH until I had one." How do you feel about that statement?

AN ADOPTION PROPOSAL

32. Johanna has a reveal-it-all approach in her adoption statement. In my experience, people with disabilities often have this approach to life. Why would Johanna and others like her habitually put everything out there? HINT: it's self-protection of some sort.

33. Have you ever been judged by someone to the degree that you felt ashamed and humiliated?

34. Have you ever judged someone to the degree that you wrote them off as "a mistake"?

35. If you could put yourself in the mindset of a potential birth mother considering giving her child for adoption, how would Johanna's adoption proposal affect you?

36. Johanna comes across as a genuinely street-wise authentic person. What role might her condition have played in shaping her into that authenticity?

THE TEXT MESSAGE

37. From the time we first meet her, Clare seems contentious and deceptive. Those are not generally viewed as noble traits in a person. Having read the story, why does Libby put up with such a person?

38. Shame plays a huge role in dragging down intimacy. What role did shame play in Clare's story?

39. Like Liliana and Johanna, Libby has a warm, positive relationship with her father. How does that line up with current views of fathers and daughters? Why do we not hear more about positive father-daughter relationships?

40. Libby could have easily lied on the witness stand. Can you explain her thinking about why she didn't?

41. Libby says, "Lesbians don't have to lie anymore." Do you agree with that?

CORRESPONDENCE

42. Dr. McDowell and his wife Trudy have what psychologists call "parental estrangement" with Clare. The problem seems to be on the increase among millennials. Why do you think that might be?

43. I carefully considered including Dr. McDowell's written response to Clare's letter home, but decided not to. Can you speculate about why I didn't feel a need to include his letter to her? HINT: I thought it would be redundant.

44. Did Clare get the punishment she deserved? More? Or Less? You decide.

45. Clare's irresponsibility caused terrible grief for many: Aoife and Aiden, Libby, Burt, and Morton. Has your irresponsibility ever brought pain to those you love?

THE MUD RUN

46. Liam has a positive outlook on his own life and the lives of others. Usually, a positive attitude is good to have, but in his case, it worked for him at times and against him at others. Describe how it works for and against him.

47. The way we love our partners is very much influenced by the relationships we have with caregivers in our

childhood and adolescence (who are usually, but not always, our biological parents). How did Maria's relationship with her parents affect her relationship with Liam?

48. Maria becomes aggressive, and less compassionate, in several aspects of her life. How would steroids fuel this kind of unmetered aggression?

49. In her eroticized mind (again, fueled by steroids), Liam is "been there, done that" as a sex partner for her. Psychologists acknowledge this as "sexual satiation," and it seems to be part of all long-term sexual relationships. Is it embarrassing to talk about the boredom/habitualness of long-term relationship sex?

50. On the same topic, some individuals prefer the "satiation" of a long-term relationship. They see satiation not as boredom, but as security—you don't have to work at it or worry about how you look. What are your thoughts? Is it boredom or security?

51. Most people think that "Liam should have put his foot down earlier or harder" with Maria. He considered being more forceful, but worried about being accused of being controlling or abusive. Are his worries legitimate? Or rationalizations?

52. Liam demanded Maria's phone and used his subversive knowledge of her password to gain access to it. Would you ever snoop through your partner's phone or personal belongings?

53. What do you think about Jaxon Ryder?

HOME TRUTHS

54. Although he disapproves with how she went about it, Father Miles says Maria's motives are pure. What does he mean by that? Would you agree?

55. Father Miles encourages Maria to apologize to Liam for her own good. How can apologizing be good for us (especially if the person we apologize to is belligerent and accusatory?)

56. "The hardest person in the world to forgive—yourself." What does Father Miles mean by that? Are you harboring guilt and shame that you need to let go of?

57. Maria says "I don't care" a total of seven times in her story. Father Miles tells her: "I don't care. The three most destructive words in the human language." Are they?

58. Have you ever felt the Urge? How did you handle it?

59. Maria says, ". . .the only person a woman isn't supposed to take care of is herself." Can you expound on that? Disagree with it?

60. Have you ever heard the expression "home truths?" Do you understand it? Is this a healthy idea?

61. Liam is all into self-respect. Many men are. Is this a male-oriented idea or can both sexes share the concern? How do women see self-respect differently than men?

LOVE YOU CAN COUNT ON

62. I have heard people say, "Love has nothing to do with money." I have mixed feelings on that. How do love

and money come together? Where do they go their separate ways?

63. Madi feels that Tony doesn't listen to her, and this has come up more than once in the book. Does this apply to men in general? Or is it just a stereotype? HINT: anthropologists say that women universally are better at verbal communication than men. How does this impact relationships between men and women?

64. Madi feels the Cold Wind of Despair more than once in this story. Where does she first feel it? What is the Cold Wind of Despair and what does it say to us about the importance of love?

65. Do you believe in angels? Why or why not? Have you ever encountered an angel? Do you know anyone who has?

66. Maria writes in Tony's medical record, "intensive care delirium has abated." Google "intensive care delirium" and consider whether it explains Tony's experience or not.

67. What was going on between Father Miles Joyce and Alexa Arioli? I still haven't figured it out!

A EULOGY IN PRAISE OF FOREVER

68. How has Tony's view of love (and life in general) been changed by Madi? What is the proper balance between materialism and spiritualism?

69. Do you believe in forever? Heaven? Nirvana? Reincarnation? Afterlife or past life?

70. Does having a spiritual view of the world help in times of crisis? If life is all material, and there is no spiritual meaning, how does one handle crises?

THE HAPPY ENDING

71. One final question, how did your feelings about yourself and someone you love change over the course of reading Cupid on Trial?

ACKNOWLEDGEMENTS

A book is never the creation of one person. Many thanks to Steven Pressfield who showed me what it means to be a writer. To Shawn Coyne who taught me how to tell a story. To Rosemary Daniels who helped me find my voice. To Tami Whitney for endless edits, and Frederick Johnson for his precise way with words. To Jane Friedman who served as a beacon. To friends, family, and followers whose names are too many to list: thank you for putting up with me during my three year obsession.

ABOUT THE AUTHOR

Dr. Brian Jory has been researching relationships, teaching about intimacy, and counseling couples for years. His theories and research studies have been published in prestigious academic journals, and have won numerous awards for their focus on spirituality and personal responsibility in relationships. Dr. Jory is a Professor at Berry College, near Atlanta, where he teaches about love, intimacy, and sexuality. He currently serves as Chair of the Education Department and as Director of the Family Studies Program. He is affiliated with the American Psychological Association, the International Family Therapy Association, and the Family Science Association of America.